50 SPECIALTY LIBRARIES OF NEW YORK CITY

T0383357

CHANDOS

INFORMATION PROFESSIONAL SERIES

Series Editor: Ruth Rikowski
(email: Rikowskigr@aol.com)

Chandos' new series of books is aimed at the busy information professional. They have been specially commissioned to provide the reader with an authoritative view of current thinking. They are designed to provide easy-to-read and (most importantly) practical coverage of topics that are of interest to librarians and other information professionals. If you would like a full listing of current and forthcoming titles, please visit www.chandospublishing.com.

New authors: we are always pleased to receive ideas for new titles; if you would like to write a book for Chandos, please contact Dr Glyn Jones on g.jones.2@elsevier.com or telephone +44 (0) 1865 843000.

50 SPECIALTY LIBRARIES OF NEW YORK CITY
From Botany to Magic

T. BALLARD

Amsterdam • Boston • Cambridge • Heidelberg
London • New York • Oxford • Paris • San Diego
San Francisco • Singapore • Sydney • Tokyo
Chandos Publishing is an imprint of Elsevier

ISBN: 978-0-08-100554-5 (print)
ISBN: 978-0-08-100560-6 (online)

British Library Cataloguing-in-Publication Data
A catalogue record for this book is available from the British Library

Library of Congress Cataloging-in-Publication Data
A catalog record for this book is available from the Library of Congress

For information on all Chandos Publishing publications
visit our website at http://store.elsevier.com/

Working together
to grow libraries in
developing countries

www.elsevier.com • www.bookaid.org

DEDICATION

The very existence of libraries affords the best evidence that we may yet have hope for the future of man

T.S. Eliot

This book is dedicated to the sixty or so librarians, directors and administrators who took time out to show me their libraries and tell me their stories. It is my hope that this will shine a much deserved spotlight on the wonderful work that you are doing.

CONTENTS

viii   Contents

ABOUT THE AUTHOR

Terry Ballard is the author of two previous books and more than 70 articles in the field of library science and is the winner of two national writing awards. Since earning his MLS in 1989 from the University of Arizona, he has worked as an academic systems librarian in New York and Connecticut. He is currently adjunct Special Projects Librarian at the College of New Rochelle in Westchester County, New York. He has presented at conferences such as *Computers in Libraries, The Third International Conference on the Book* in Oxford, and the *American Library Association*. He is also the author of *Google this: Putting Google and other social media sites to work for your library* (Chandos, 2012).

FOREWORD

When Terry Ballard invited me to write the foreword to his new book, *Fifty Specialty Libraries in New York City*, I knew I would be reflecting on Terry as a personality, not just the organization and writing of the book. In the 20-plus years I have known Terry, from the first time I met him at a Library and Information Technology Association conference, I could not imagine any time with him that would not be unique, joyful, and educational. When he came to my library school research methods class as a guest lecturer, he inspired my students to do some of their most creative work. This was especially true following the lecture based on his book *Google This*.

His approach to life and to this book is positive and inquisitive. Unlike most library directories, this one has a personal approach as well as a careful evaluation of each library. The pronoun "I" is used often. If you want a quick description of a library, this is not it. Instead, you will experience Terry's eye-opening, thorough inspection and assessment of each library. Before you visit, you will know if this is a library you will like. Feeling and tone are as much a part of each description as is the size of the collection or the number of rooms in the library.

The libraries were selected after an examination of directories and a search of the Internet as well as from the author's own knowledge of libraries. Of the 50 libraries, some are part of larger institutions such as The Berg Collection at The New York Public Library, while others are smaller and/or freestanding libraries such as the Kristine Mann Library, a library devoted to the works of Carl Jung.

If you like the author's approach, each entry will be a delight to read, whether or not you visit the library. The detailed descriptions are enhanced by photographs taken by Terry, for whom photography is a serious avocation, and include information such as the extensive history of each library. The descriptions all follow a similar pattern, beginning with directions on how to find the library, not always easy in a city like New York. Terry's sense of openness, discovery, and good humor infuses each library description. His keen observation skills are evident in all entries. After reading this book, you will feel like you have been in each library and need to visit only to see how closely your observations match Terry's. You will also have a good notion of whether a specific library is likely to be useful for your own research.

This book is perfect for the armchair library traveler, the library visitor, and the researcher of special subjects. I have not seen another book like it and doubt I ever will. So, read, visit, enjoy, and find the information you desire in one or more of these very special libraries.

—by Pauline Rothstein, a New York-based library consultant and previous academic library director

PREFACE

Like a lot of good stories, this book starts with a dog. A friend of mine named Marilyn Johnson wrote a book called *This Book Is Overdue!* She had been an obituary writer and noticed that the most interesting obits were from departed librarians, so she decided to embed herself in the world of librarians and learn what makes us tick. One of the libraries she visited was the American Kennel Club library in New York City. When I read that, I thought "I didn't know there was a library devoted to dogs in New York. What other libraries could there be?" Once I started looking into it, the list grew precipitously. I could identify more than 35, and I figured there must be at least 50. There are. I also speculated that these lesser-known libraries are run by people who have a story to tell and who want their library to be better known than it is.

So I devised a plan. I would visit 50 libraries in Manhattan; write about what I see, what the librarians have to say about their institutions, and how to get there on public transportation; and take a few pictures. I would ask each library a series of simple questions such as "What is your source of funding?" "How long has your library been in existence?" "What online catalog do you use?" "Dewey, Library of Congress, or homemade?" "What are your accomplishments or plans for digitization?" "Who is the most famous person to use your library?" (Hint—there were some amazing answers.) "What do you consider to be your flagship holding?"

I put the idea out to a few publishers—one of them thought about it for a year and then passed. Too New York. Too library. Then, in a great stroke of luck, Chandos, who had published my last book, was expanding their repertoire of library writing, and my editor George Knott encouraged me to send a proposal. Around Thanksgiving week I got the go-ahead and began to map out the particulars. Chandos had wanted me to expand the scope a bit and cover all five boroughs. This turned out to be an easy change, although I had a hard time with Staten Island.

Over the next months I visited libraries in all circumstances. Some were barely holding on, and some were fabulously well endowed. The most important requirement for inclusion in this book is access. The library has to be available to interested members of the public, even though about half of them require an advance appointment. For this reason, most academic libraries were left out. There were more law libraries open to the public than I could cover, but medical libraries were nearly impossible to find. As I went along with my visits, I added new libraries to the list—the best suggestions came from the visited libraries. Several librarians pointed out that the American Society for Psychical Research had a library on the Upper West Side.

As the winter stretched into the spring of 2015 I found that the plan of visiting 50 libraries could be a bit grueling for a senior citizen, but one important thing kept me going. The enthusiasm for this project among the visited librarians was a wonder. I have heard many people say "I can't wait to get a copy of this book. What a great idea!"

A few friends had pointed out that there were already directories of special libraries in New York. I found this news to be less than compelling, because I knew that the book I write will have a far more interesting tone than, say, the phone book. This will be filled with a series of "wow" moments, such as holding a piece of balsa wood from the *Kon-Tiki* and seeing Mark Twain's pool cue, e.e. cummings's desk, and Helen Keller's Oscar statuette. At the Louis Armstrong archive, I got to hold Satchmo's trumpet. At the Morgan Library I held a long letter from Mark Twain to his publisher explaining how he got his pseudonym. I also learned why there is a secret shelf in Morgan's private office. Just a block away from the Morgan, I brought the project full circle by visiting the American Kennel Club library.

The book is the result of the stars lining up in my life. As I approach the year 2016 it will mark the 50th anniversary of my first job in a library. I joined the Phoenix Public Library in September of 1966 as a very junior part-time clerk, and then became a paraprofessional. In 1989 I took advantage of a satellite program from the University of Arizona in Tucson and got my MLS. I'm told that the motto of the University of Arizona library school is "Get your library degree and see the world." In my case it was New York. We rented out our house, packed up the dog, and moved 2300 miles north and east. During the next 25 years I enjoyed a career that was everything I could have imagined.

That leads to the second Valentine in this book—New York. When we first moved to Long Island in 1990 the plan was to spend two or three years making a reputation, which I could ride to better job opportunities in Arizona. Then something strange happened. New York got its hooks into me. I had always been a Mets fan, but now we started getting swept up in Yankee resurgence. I found that I was more suited to academic librarianship than public, and there was an enormous selection of colleges and universities in the area. After working 24 years in one library I found it refreshing to try new things every few years.

New York is, quite simply, a cultural treasure chest. Early in our time here, we saw Pavarotti sing and Tom Robbins read in Central Park. We stood on the banks of the East River in 1994 to see the regatta of boats celebrating the 500th anniversary of Columbus's voyage. At the New York Public Library we saw the Dead Sea Scrolls. At the Morgan Library we saw a Gutenberg Bible for the first time. We saw live national broadcasts of *The Today Show*. At the Book Expo conferences in the spring we saw too many authors to remember, but my favorite moment was making Michael Moore laugh. Two years in New York stretched into five, then 10, then 25.

So now I offer my view of the New York City Library world. I hope that you will find a library or two that you cannot wait to visit. After writing about technology for years, I hope that this will provide information that is more enduring. These are all libraries that have survived through the economic crash of 2008 and Hurricane Sandy, so I think they are in it for the long haul. In most cases, I want to go back myself, when I'm not in a hurry, and savor the joys to be found in these enduring libraries.

INTRODUCTION

Two years ago I was at the doctor's office with my wife. We mentioned that we both were librarians, as was our son.

"I'm sorry to hear that," he said.

We were not sure why he would be, so we probed further. It turns out that despite his great knowledge about medicine, he is one of those people who believe that all human knowledge is on the Internet and that libraries are doomed. In his view it is a good thing that we are near retirement age, so we do not have to wait out the final chapter.

The next year I got my chance to write this book and visit 50 libraries in the city of New York. Nearly half of them have been in operation for 100 years or more. It gave me a unique vantage point to take the pulse of libraries in my city. Some are struggling, to be sure, but others are fabulously successful at navigating the world of information in a time of unprecedented change.

You cannot overstate the extent of the revolution. Years ago, I wanted to look at the lyrics to a song. Since I worked at a large public library, it should not have been hard to find what I needed. I was directed to a catalog case filled with index cards that had been lovingly maintained for decades. I found my song, but it was mentioned in only one book. That book had gone missing, so that was the end of my quest for the time being.

Ten years later I had a rather amusing exchange with a friend of mine who just could not warm up to this computer world. He told me that we could not compare the Internet age to the Gutenberg Revolution. Why not? Because Gutenberg's printing press empowered people to get their message out in ways that were not open to them in the past.

If anything, today's revolution empowers people too well. A year ago I was teaching a class of information literacy to a group of adults who were returning to higher education after starting careers in New York City. They had the belief that Google checked its information for accuracy before indexing it. To prove how wrong that was, I added the nonsense phrase "Sarah Palin can see the planet Jupiter from her back porch" into my own Website. While literally true (anybody can see the planet from their back porch), it did not add to humanity's wealth of information. Nonetheless, it showed up in Google five days later.

Most libraries in New York are managing to provide traditional services of books and archive materials while, to some extent, joining the digital world. As the librarians in these institutions told me their stories, I was prouder than ever to be a part of this profession.

CHAPTER 1

The Pioneers: Three Subscription Libraries, 440 Years of Service to New York

Libraries are reservoirs of strength, grace and wit, reminders of order, calm and continuity, lakes of mental energy, neither warm nor cold, light nor dark.
Germaine Greer

Young Samuel Clemens, on a quest to see all of the cities in America that he had read about in books, visited New York in 1853 and soon found work as a printer's assistant at one of New York's many publishing companies. He took lodging at a boarding house on Duane Street and spent evenings at a library that had been established for young workers to better their lot in life through learning. As far as we can tell that library did not survive into modern times, but three libraries from that time did. It has not always been easy, but the three institutions are very proud of their history and their tenacity, serving New Yorkers through the Civil War, World Wars I and II, the Great Depression, the 2008 Mess, and Hurricane Sandy. It was a special treat to visit them and listen to their stories.

THE NEW YORK SOCIETY LIBRARY

Address: 53 East 79th Street, New York, NY 10075
URL: https://www.nysoclib.org/
Telephone: (212) 288-6900
E-mail: reference@nysoclib.org
Access: Full access for members; public access to collections onsite and most events
Facebook: https://www.facebook.com/nysoclib
Twitter: https://twitter.com/nysoclib
YouTube: https://www.youtube.com/user/nysoclib
Transportation: No. 6 train to 77th Street; bus line 1, 2, 3, or 4 to 79th Street

50 Specialty Libraries of New York City
ISBN 978-0-08-100554-5

Early in this project, I was impressed with the fact that I would be covering two libraries that were almost 200 years old. Later I would find out to my great surprise that a third library had already celebrated its 250 birthday. The New York Society Library, founded in 1754, needed a charter from King George III to begin its enterprise.

Library main entrance.

Owing to a bizarre mix-up with e-mail, I was not able to reach them until one day before my visit, but they were very generous with their time, given the short notice. I first spoke with Carolyn Waters, Assistant Head Librarian, who was working the reference desk when I came in. She began to fill me in on the illustrious history of this library, which is the fifth oldest in America. It has been in continuous operation, except for a hiatus during the Revolutionary War. Afterward, when New York emerged as the capitol of the new country, its membership included a Who's Who of founding fathers: John Jay and John Adams were members. Alexander Hamilton and Aaron Burr were both members, but probably did not use the library at the same time. The library is particularly proud of something they found in their old circulation records—a notation of a book being checked out by George Washington.

Obviously, my standard question about which celebrity had used the library was completely absurd here. Washington Irving and Clement Moore were trustees, and members included John James Audubon, Herman Melville, and Willa Cather. In the case of Melville, he had checked out a book covering Arctic regions and whale fishing prior to writing *Moby-Dick*. In their 2004 book *The New York Society Library: 250 Years*, there are testimonials from Arthur Schlesinger, Jacques Barzun, Susan Cheever, Dominick Dunne, and Wendy Wasserstein. Ralph Waldo Emerson was not a member, but he was a featured speaker here.

The library has resided at its current location since 1937, when the library retrofitted the 1917 John S. Rogers mansion, which is now a New York City landmark. The original location was in City Hall, and the library spent more than 80 years on University Place. I was taken on a tour of the building, courtesy of Sara Holliday, Events Coordinator and Head Librarian's Assistant. I learned that the library has 300,000 volumes and that they are kept in Dewey order. I also complimented them on maintaining their records in an Innovative Interfaces catalog, as this is the sure sign of a prosperous library.

We started with the reference room on the first floor. It is notable for that twentieth century library staple—a card catalog. It is still accurate, but has not been fed for some time. This is the portion of the library that is available to all interested citizens, and it contains a basic ready reference collection of things like dictionaries and encyclopedias. The circulation desk was already humming with business from people who could afford the $320 family membership fee—a full list of membership options can be found on their Web site. These fees, plus an endowment, are the principal means of support for the library. As we made our way through the floors I saw a thriving Children's Library. Just past that on the third floor there is a members-only reading room for people who really need peace and quiet. The larger members-only reading room is on the second floor. The fourth floor is a staff-only area and the fifth floor has a section with six private rooms devoted to working authors. We tiptoed through the halls here to confirm that serious concentration was going on behind closed doors.

Members-only reading room.

The author rooms have a mythology all their own. Wendy Wasserstein claimed that she wrote almost all of *The Heidi Chronicles* on 79th Street. Other modern authors in the corral include Roald Dahl, Leonard Bernstein, Lewis Mumford, Edward Gorey, P.G. Wodehouse, Barbara Tuchman, Brendan Gill (who also served as a trustee), and Willa Cather. This is one very proud institution. Yet, I had to admit that when I began the list of target libraries I was unaware of the library. Holliday admitted that it is not as well known as they would like it to be, so they welcomed efforts like mine to spread the word.

I met Mark Bartlett, the Head Librarian, and we exchanged cards in his office overlooking 79th Street. Then Holliday and I moved on to the upper floors. These are all members-only spaces, and the main one looks like the nineteenth century Parisian reading rooms of your dreams. Also on the second floor we saw the current exhibition of books with extra writing on their pages—at the hands of famous authors. I gravitated to a copy of George Bernard Shaw's *Too True to Be Good*, significant because, even though it was a minor play, it featured his friend T.E. Lawrence as a thinly disguised character. This was a sample from a Special Collections Department containing more than 12,000 rare books.

An old friend of mine from New York University mentioned that, after she retires, she wants to volunteer at The New York Society Library. I told her that she had chosen well.

GENERAL SOCIETY OF MECHANICS AND TRADESMEN LIBRARY

Address: 20 West 44th Street, New York, NY 10036
URL: http://generalsociety.org/?page_id=103
Facebook: https://www.facebook.com/pages/General-Society-Library/238365909558261?ref=br_tf
Twitter: https://twitter.com/generalsociety
E-mail: info@generalsociety.org
Access: Open to members for a nominal fee
Transportation: Bus–No. 3 or 4 Madison or 5th; subway–B, D, F, or M to Bryant Park

One day early in the project, I was early for an appointment to a Midtown library, and I noticed that the General Society Library was just a block away, so I took a chance and dropped in on them. The security guard told me that they were closed at the moment, but said I should talk to Karin Taylor upstairs. I did go up and introduced myself and explained the project. When I had first thought of this book, I was impressed and surprised that there were subscription libraries still going after more than 150 years, so this library was particularly important to me. Karin was immediately supportive, going so far as to open up the reading room below and giving me access to take pictures of this wonderful old building.

Several weeks later I came back for my official visit, talking with Society Executive Director Victoria Dengel as well as Karin. We sat at a long hardwood table underneath a bust of Andrew Carnegie, and they filled me in on a history that encompassed four centuries. The Society was founded in 1785 to help with the working conditions and general welfare of young tradesmen and their families. The library came along in 1820 to help with the self-education of workers who could never afford traditional higher education, and evolved over the years into a general circulating library. The library followed a traditional pattern of moves—beginning in Lower Manhattan and eventually occupying its current building in 1899, with a generous assist from General Society member Andrew Carnegie.

I asked them a standard question about which famous person had used their library and got a wealth of responses, starting with the notables who had given speeches to the organization. These included Ralph Waldo Emerson, Horace Greeley, and Admiral Robert Peary. Library members included Isaac Asimov and Garrison Keillor. The Old World charm of the building has led to using the facility for filming, and one notable guest for this purpose was Robin Williams. "He had a star trailer parked in front, but he spent a lot of time looking in the library and asking questions," remembers Dengel. Walking through the building later, I was shown the Members Assembly room that had been used in filming the Robin Williams movie.

Main reading room of the Society Library.

They told me that there are about 100,000 volumes in the collection, including their legacy collection of pre-1923 volumes. The year 1923 is famous for being the cutoff year for public domain—anything older can be digitized and shared without fear. I asked, but was told that digitization plans are not on their immediate radar. Also they have a major collection of fiction from 1923 to 1950. The earliest books still use a classification scheme devised by the Society's librarian at the turn of the twentieth century. More modern titles are now arranged in Library of Congress order. In modern times, the library was given ownership of the Crouse Library for Publishing Arts. The online catalog is run on a system called Softlink.

The John M. Mossman Lock Collection.

The collection the Society is most proud of is on the top floor, overlooking the reading room. It is the John M. Mossman Lock Museum, containing locks dating back to 4000 BC and extending to modern safe locks. On the wall past the locks are the portraits of past presidents of the Society. One of them is Victoria Dengel's father, which helps to explain how this organization is in her DNA. I asked them where they send researchers to lunch and was told that the Red Flame is the eatery of choice for its quality and variety. If users are in a hurry then they are directed to several delis on 43rd Street.

Society banner over the reading room.

A few months later, my wife and I were honored to attend an event celebrating artisanship and the founding of the Society by 22 craftsmen 230 years ago. The General Society of Mechanics and Tradesmen of the City of New York continues to honor its original theme, By Hammer and Hand All Arts Do Stand. And that night they declared the Society "The Home of the Artisan." The crowd was a prosperous-looking group of people, young and old, who were getting things done in New York City. The evening included remarks by architect Peter Pennoyer and Master Artisan Jean Wiart. Dengel got up to speak, and it is clear that she has every intention of steering the society toward its 250th anniversary in good stead.

LIBRARY: THE CENTER FOR FICTION

Address: 17 East 47th Street, New York, NY
URL: http://www.centerforfiction.org/
Telephone: (212) 755-6710
E-mail: info@centerforfiction.org
Access: Basic membership $150; otherwise limited access to the public
Facebook: https://www.facebook.com/thecenterforfiction
Twitter: @Center4Fiction

The Center for Fiction began as the Mercantile Library and has been retooled in modern times as a nonprofit educational institution. Like the General Society of Mechanics and Tradesmen, it began library operations in 1820.

The Center is located in Midtown, just east of the Diamond District. If you are not paying close attention to the street numbers, it is easy to walk right past it—I know, because I did. The entry to the Center looks like a used book store, but the real treasures for book lovers are on the higher floors, which only members may access.

I met Matt Nelson, the library manager, who was quick to point out that he is not a trained librarian. On the other hand, he spends his time away from the center running something called the Gentle Pages, a subscription library in Brooklyn that has a core membership of 500 subscribers. Nelson promises that the Center will hire a librarian in the near future to lead the institution through some major changes. Judging by the highly positive reviews on Yelp, Nelson was doing just fine.

By this time, I had ascended in every type of elevator imaginable, but the Center has an elevator car with catalog cards and newspaper clippings as floor-to-ceiling wallpaper, so you cannot help but be in the spirit. On the second floor there is an elegant reading room with a view to 47th Street.

Center for Fiction Reading Room.

Higher up, we found the book stacks. As the Center's name would suggest, the main menu item here is fiction (particularly mysteries and suspense), but there is some nonfiction and that is kept in Dewey order. I was told that the catalog is run on Follett software, which is PC based.

A floor of the Center for Fiction provides members with work space for writing.

In its almost 200-year history, the Center has seen its share of famous authors. I was told that Edgar Allen Poe and Mark Twain were part of the story, but the 47th Street location has been used only since 1930. The page of videos showing recent programs is fairly impressive as well, with contributions by Elmore Leonard and Joyce Carol Oates. Nelson is particularly proud of the Center's association with author Gordon Lish, who is also an editor and a teacher of writing, known for his boot-camp tactics.

FURTHER READING

Atlas Obscura article about the Mossman Lock Collection: http://www.atlasobscura.com/places/john-m-mossman-lock-collection.

Behind the scenes at the General Society of Mechanics and Tradesmen: http://untappedcities.com/2013/07/10/behind-the-scenes-at-the-general-society-of-mechanics-tradesmen-the-second-oldest-library-in-nyc/.

Crouse Library for Publishing Arts: http://en.wikipedia.org/wiki/Crouse_Library_for_Publishing_Arts.

Guardian article about George Washington's overdue books: http://www.theguardian.com/world/2010/apr/18/george-washington-library-new-york.

Hidden Libraries of New York City: http://www.atlasobscura.com/articles/secret-libraries-of-new-york-city.

Interview with architect Peter Pennoyer: http://newyorkyimby.com/2014/04/interview-with-the-architect-peter-pennoyer.html.

Interview with Gordon Lish: http://www.thegiganticmag.com/magazine/articleDetail.
php?p=articleDetail&id=108.

New York Review of Books article about exhibit at the New York Society Library of
books with handwritten notes by famous authors: http://www.nybooks.com/blogs/
gallery/2015/feb/19/marginalia-insults-epiphanies/.

New York Times article: http://www.nytimes.com/2010/03/07/realestate/07streets.html?_
r=0.

Videos of past programs at the Center for fiction: http://www.centerforfiction.org/
audiovideo/video/.

Wikipedia article about the New York Society Library: https://en.wikipedia.org/wiki/
New_York_Society_Library.

Yelp review of Center for Fiction: http://www.yelp.com/biz/the-center-for-fiction-new-
york-2.

Zoominfo page about Victoria Dengel: http://www.zoominfo.com/p/Victoria-Dengel/
1160509024.

CHAPTER 2

Economics

A wise man should have money in his head but not his heart.

Jonathan Swift

AMERICAN NUMISMATIC SOCIETY—THE HARRY W. BASS JR. LIBRARY

Address: 75 Varick Street, 11th floor, New York, NY 10013
URL: http://numismatics.org/Library/Library
Telephone: (212) 571-4470
Access: Members: Free. Government photo ID required.
Nonmembers: $20 per day. Photo ID required.
Students with valid student ID: Free.
Facebook: https://www.facebook.com/AmericanNumismaticSociety
Twitter: https://twitter.com/ANSCoins
Transportation: Subway–1, 2 line at Canal Street.

Like millions of little boys in the 1950s, I was an avid collector of coins, usually pennies. At that time, coins from the 1930s were readily found on the streets of Phoenix, and we could fill jars with that wartime curiosity of lead pennies (now impossibly rare). If you went to the bank and bought a roll of pennies, you could often find something even older, such as a 1909 first issue of Lincoln. Then you replaced that with a modern penny and brought it right back to the bank teller, who loved this little operation (at least they never told us otherwise, but there were pained expressions on their faces). Then you learned the rest of this game, sadly. I once amassed a good stack of buffalo nickels and took it to the coin store in central Phoenix. The man scratched his chin and said there is nothing much of interest here, but he would take them off my hands for 7 cents each. A month later, I saw them in a jar by the door: "Rare nickels: 75 cents each." That ended my lifetime dealings with coin stores.

50 Specialty Libraries of New York City
ISBN 978-0-08-100554-5

Main reading room of the library.

Still, I was happy to add the American Numismatic Society's library to my list in the first round. It was the second library I visited after getting my contract. I had contacted David Hill, who was very prompt in getting back to me and setting up a January visit. The building is a high-rise about a block north of Canal Street. The process of visiting reminded me of visiting a bank vault. The hallway leading up to the library was very sleek, with displays of the organization's long history. It began in 1858, and they purchased the first book for the library a year later. Unlike nearly all of the older libraries in this book, the Numismatic Society began in Midtown and then moved to the far north of Manhattan in 1908, as part of the complex created by Archer Huntington, founder of the Hispanic Society. In 1864, shortly after their founding, they added Archaeology to their name, but by 1908 they had gone back to their original roots. They have been at their current location since 2008.

David's title is the Francis D. Campbell Librarian, an endowed position named after the man who worked for the library for 50 years and as librarian for 30 of those. Hill told me that he still gets calls asking for Campbell, who was, at the time of my visit, still alive but very much retired. The typical users are students, scholars, and collectors. There are more than 100,000 volumes, with a substantial collection of the society's own publications. When I asked which item they were proudest of holding, I was told that they kept a book in honor of Ulysses S. Grant. It is a two-volume scrapbook put together by George Kunz of Tiffany & Co. having to do with ceremonies and a medal produced by the Numismatic Society for Grant's Tomb. The library's rare book room also contains *De Asse et Partibus Euis*, by Guillaume Budé, 1516 (Roman B833 P37), on Roman coinage and one of the earliest books, if not the first, devoted to the study of ancient coins.

As we looked through the rarest or the rare, it somehow came up that we were both fans of the Grateful Dead. He had followed the band to many concerts. I have been to only one, but I did create a highly specialized Web page for Deadhead librarians.

I spent some time looking through their online catalog and found that it contained very deep coverage of the library's substantial holdings of journal articles. Its name, DONUM, is an acronym for "Database of Numismatic Materials" and is also the Latin word for "gift." There were numerous references to journal articles printed 40 and 50 years ago. The library also provides links to MANTIS, an online database that catalogs the thousands of coins in the organization's vaults.

LIBRARY: FOUNDATION CENTER

Address: 32 Old Slip, 24th Floor, New York, NY 10005-3500
URL: http://foundationcenter.org/newyork/library.html
Telephone: (212) 620-4230
E-mail: http://foundationcenter.org/getstarted/askus/
Access: Open to the public
Facebook: https://www.facebook.com/foundationcenter?fref=ts
Twitter: https://twitter.com/FCNewYork

I had a brief experience when I visited one of the Foundation Center's funding agencies sometime in the 1990s to give a talk about XML. The office was high in a tall building with a stunning view out to the East River. I had been in contact with the library director Jimmy Tom for several weeks, and we managed to set up a Friday morning meeting in March.

I found out that, like many of these libraries, they use Koha for their online catalog, with ByWater as their automation facilitator. By way of explanation, Koha is an open access program, so it is free to any library who wants to use it. However, it requires a level of automation competence that most small libraries lack, so nearly all of them sign up with a company that guides them through the process and manages their technical support. Tom told me that the library owns 5000 volumes, and most of these are monographs rather than serial sets. I had observed an information session about Koha when a nearby library was migrating several years ago, and it seemed that the basic bibliographic information was well served, but name authority was still a weak link. Tom did not dispute this point. The library does its own cataloging and uses a home-made system rather than Dewey or Library of Congress. According to Tom, "We are particularly proud of *The Foundation Center's Guide to Proposal Writing*, now in its sixth edition. It is written by Jane Geever and incorporates results of interviews with grantmakers across the nation."

Free materials from the library.

Tom filled me in on the history of his parent organization. Foundations including the Rockefeller, Carnegie, Kellogg, and Russell Sage created the Center in 1956. The founding president, F. Emerson Andrews, came from the Sage Foundation. The original mission was to create a "strategic gathering place for knowledge about foundations." The Center soon became national in scope, opening offices in major cities around the country. For its national program, it gathers information from sources such as Web pages, IRS reports, and direct contact. By now it devotes much of its effort in gathering data from around the world.

Research area of the library.

The Foundation Center is heavily into the use of social media. In addition to the usual outlets such as Facebook, Twitter, and YouTube, they instruct each regional office to create a blog. The New York office has a staff of five, and they are all involved in training, reference, and special programs for the public and for agencies. Their online product, Foundation Directory Online, is available for as little as $399 per year for people who need the information but are not conveniently close to a library that subscribes. People in New York do not have that problem. In addition to the Foundation Center itself, the New York Public Library subscribes and makes the full database available at the Stephen A. Schwarzman Building. The Bronx Library Center and the St. George Library Center are part of the Funding Information Network, a network of libraries, community foundations, and other nonprofit resource centers that provide access to Foundation Center databases and publications.

Circulation desk of the library.

While the library is primarily reference, Tom told me that the library does a limited number of two-week circulations to registered members. The real activity here seems to be in programming. He gave me the March calendar, and I saw that there was training scheduled for 15 days. All-day sessions involved a fee, but the one-hour sessions were free—you just need to schedule a slot. Most of the 50 libraries were involved in grantsmanship, so this library is appropriate to all of the others.

FURTHER READING

American Numismatic Society Magazine: http://ansmagazine.com/.
DEADUCATED – a web page for librarians who are fans of the Grateful Dead: http://www.terryballard.org/deadlib/.
Foundation Directory Online: https://subscribe.foundationcenter.org/fdo.
Frank Campbell and the ANS Library: An appreciation: http://www.coinbooks.org/esylum_v11n31a09.html.
Investor's Guide to United States Coins: https://books.google.com/books?id=lk9sgCd_FF8C&lpg=PA25&dq=american%20numismatic%20society%20library&pg=PA25#v=onepage&q=american%20numismatic%20society%20library&f=false.
Mantis Catalog of coin holdings: http://numismatics.org/search/.
Russell Sage Foundation 100 year document: http://www.russellsage.org/sites/all/files/u4/Brief%20History%20of%20RSF.pdf.
Wikipedia page about American Numismatic Society: https://en.wikipedia.org/wiki/American_Numismatic_Society.
Wikipedia page about the Foundation Center: https://en.wikipedia.org/wiki/Foundation_Center.

CHAPTER 3

Law Libraries

I learned law so well, the day I graduated I sued the college, won the case, and got my tuition back.

Fred Allen

Of my 50 years in library school, five of them were spent in academic law libraries. I had computer skills, particularly in online catalogs, that made up for my total cluelessness about legal scholarship. This is a common situation in law libraries, where the reference librarians usually have their doctorates in law and the technical services people do their technical thing. You may be curious about someone who spent three grueling years learning the law and then did not practice it. I was curious, but the common answer is that they did not really want to practice and were happy to have a good steady career for life.

NEW YORK COUNTY COURTS PUBLIC ACCESS LAW LIBRARY

Address: 80 Centre Street, New York, NY
Telephone: (646) 386–3715, current information line at (646) 386–3713
E-mail: rparenti@nycourts.gov
Access: Reference library available to the public

According to Library Director Richard Parenti, state law mandates that each county provide a public access law library for its citizens. I made an unannounced visit to the library in January 2015 when I was in Lower Manhattan to see the American Society of Numismatics Library. Subways are somewhat near, but still entail a bit of a walk. The nearest subway is a 5-minute walk to the No. 6 station at Lafayette and Canal Street or south to the City Hall station. These are best if you are heading to Grand Central. If you want to go directly to Penn Station, it is a 10-minute walk northwest to the Canal Street station of the A, C, and E lines or the Franklin Street station on the No. 1 line. There are bus lines in the area serving Worth Street, but past experience has been that they are as rare in Tribeca as Red

Sox fans. The building is an imposing marble structure that was built during the reign of Governor Al Smith.

After going through intense scrutiny at security, I took the elevator up to the fourth floor and made my way to the northeast corner of the building. I talked to the assistant, who told me that the director would be in soon, so I looked around to get the feel of the place. The library is neatly kept, with its estimated 5000 volumes in ranges of uniformly bound legal volumes. Along the south window, facing Worth Street, there is a table loaded with current issues of New York law newspapers. There are a dozen or so long wood tables, and there were several patrons seated around the room, intent on legal discovery. In the east window, there is a view to Columbus Park, an area that is much better known for its previous name—Five Points.

Research area facing Worth Street.

I sat down at one of the public computer stations and found them to be well equipped with databases, including Lexis, WestLaw, New York Courts Database, Loislaw, and New York Law Journal. Printing is 25 cents per page.

Eventually, Library Director Richard Parenti arrived, and we made plans for me to make a formal visit, which happened about two months later. This time when I went through security, the guards confiscated my cameras, since the building contains a number of courtrooms, and cameras are not allowed in New York courts. I decided to stay quiet about that and just see what Parenti wanted. He thought that I should definitely be able to take pictures, so he called his boss, and worked his way up the chain of command until a decision was made much higher up that I should be allowed to take a few pictures, as I had done at every library but one so far. Minutes later, the captain of the guard himself came up to deliver my cameras. There were smiles all around.

Richard Parenti, library director.

Richard is a quiet and intense man with a somewhat understated sense of humor. He told me that the library has been going for a bit more than 10 years—founded shortly after the state mandated that every county maintain a law library with full access to the public. This access is a very big thing to Parenti, who told me that lawyers usually have well-stocked libraries in their agencies, but working citizens with legal problems have far fewer options for information. However, there are limits—"We don't do any reference over the telephone."

When I was in library school, our main professor drove one thing into our heads: "Librarians are the bridge between people and the information they need." This seems to come second nature to Parenti, as he showed me a flyer that is handed to would-be patrons who visit the library after hours. It gives the addresses and phone numbers of other law libraries in the area with longer hours, such as the legal collection at the New York Public Library Business and Industry Library on 34th Street.

Beyond that, he also wrote the *New York City Legal Assistance Handbook*, which aspires to be a source for any question a person would have when embarking on a legal reference quest in the city.

I asked about any famous persons who had used the library, but he said that most famous people would tend to send surrogates in to do their research for them, but that one had been somebody accused of supplying drugs to a movie star who had died of an overdose.

He had a more ready answer when I asked about the library's flagship holding. He went over to the ready reference shelf and pulled out a copy of West's volume of landlord/tenant law in New York. "This is something that gets used virtually every day here. Judges specifically recommend this library as a place for combatants to get this kind of information."

I asked which system they use for their online catalog and was told that it was supplied by OCLC. Importantly, since the library has no Web page that I could find, access to the catalog was available only to users inside the library.

LIBRARY: QUEENS SUPREME COURT LAW LIBRARY

Address: 88-11 Sutphin Boulevard, Room 65, Jamaica, NY 11435
URL: https://www.nycourts.gov/library/queens/
Telephone: (718) 298-1206
E-mail: law_library_queens@courts.state.ny.us
Access: Open to the public
Transportation: LIRR Jamaica station, E subway line three blocks south of the library, or F subway line, Sutphin Avenue station, two blocks north of the library

This library is on an upper floor in the county courthouse, and past experience had told me that I might not be able to take pictures, and this turned out to be true. On the other hand, I got a good feeling about the visit when the policeman who was working security at the entrance went out of his way to tell me what a great library this is. Despite the fact that I visited on relatively short notice, librarians Denise Naya and Kellie Adams were very helpful in giving me all the information I needed. I was told that the library had been run for decades by a librarian who retired just a few years ago, and it was a shame he was not around to talk to me.

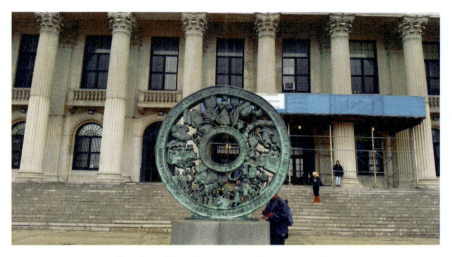

Exterior of the Queens courthouse complex.

It was a shame about photography, because this was one of the more attractive law libraries that I have seen. A sign outside the door makes sure that there is no doubt that everyone is welcome in this library.

As you walk in, there is a circulation desk in the center of the room, and the reference desk is past that, along the windows facing Manhattan to the west. The room is very neatly arranged, with reports from all states shelved along the north side of the room and an equal area of New York materials. On the south side, they keep treatises and regional reports. I was told that the volume count was about 100,000, arranged in Library of Congress order. Of this, there was no one volume they could point to as their most prized possession.

To the right of the reference desk, there are several terminals providing a generous selection of legal tools, including LexisNexis, Westlaw, Loislaw, and HeinOnline. Sirsi/Dynix is the vendor for their online catalog, which includes a smartphone application for frequent searchers. A link at the bottom says that you can use this to search the catalog on Facebook and on a smartphone application, but those did not work on the day I tried them.

With its pleasant Old World look and wood paneling, the library is the image of what a law library should look like, so it is no surprise that it has been used to film motion pictures in the past. In answer to the question about famous visitors, I was told that they were visited by Burt Pugach, a lawyer who hired men to throw lye in the face of his ex-fiancée Linda Riss. He was convicted and served 16 years in prison. When he was released, he married Riss, even though the attack had left her blind in one eye and seriously impaired in the other. Their story inspired the film *Crazy Love*.

Even though the laws mandating county law libraries did not begin until 1946, the Queens library had begun years before in Long Island City. The current building was a product of the Works Progress Administration. With its Greco-Roman exterior, it is a major signpost for people arriving at the Jamaica railway station from the west. The librarians told me that there had been a subtle shift in usership over the years. It used to be visited overwhelmingly by lawyers, but lately there were a lot more people getting the information they needed to represent themselves. Since much of the library specialty is current legal information, there is little in the way of digitization here.

I noticed that the reference desk held a Mets figurine as a point of local pride; Ms. Adams admitted that she was a Red Sox fan.

FURTHER READING

Burt Pugach Wikipedia page: http://en.wikipedia.org/wiki/Burt_Pugach.
Burt & Linda Pugach's book: "A very different love story:" http://www.amazon.com/very-different-love-story-intimate/dp/0688030890/.
Daniel Finkelstein; Lucas A Ferrara. (1997). West's New York practice series, F, G. St. Paul, Minn, West Pub. Co.
Floor map of the library: https://www.nycourts.gov/library/queens/FloorMap/tour/tour_main.htm.
NOLO catalog of legal information http://www.nolo.com/.

CHAPTER 4

Medicine

Beware of medical books. You may die of a misprint.

Mark Twain

NEW YORK ACADEMY OF MEDICINE

Location: 1216 Fifth Avenue at 103rd Street, New York, NY 10029
URL: http://www.nyam.org/#sthash.D0nr4Fdw.dpuf
Library Catalog: http://www.nyam.org/library/
Blog: http://nyamcenterforhistory.org/
Facebook: https://www.facebook.com/nyamnyc
E-mail: library@nyam.org
Telephone: (212) 822-7315
Transportation: Bus line 3 or 4

This was the first library I visited since getting the contract to write this book, so I was eager to get it right. I got in on the early train to Penn Station, and the day famous for drenching rain, so I took the No. 4 bus from 32nd Street, which made its torturous way up Madison Avenue to 103rd Street—a journey that took about 45 minutes and got me to the door right on time. If I had been in more of a hurry I would have walked two blocks farther east to Lexington Avenue and taken the subway uptown.

New York Academy of Medicine (NYAM) is a grand marble building on 5th Avenue, but the entrance is actually on 103rd Street. While waiting to be seen, I sat at a table in a pleasant coffee shop that is off the lobby of the academy. I was met by Arlene Shaner, Reference Librarian for Historical Collections, Center for the History of Medicine and Public Health, and Anne Garner, Library Curator. Arlene had been working at the library for decades and turned out to have a considerable knowledge of the other libraries on my target list. Anne was younger and had recently joined NYAM after working at the Metropolitan Museum.

Access to the public must be prearranged, but Shaner said that they schedule a number of visits for graduate students, undergraduates, writers, and lay people of all stripes. They do NOT serve people on a self-diagnosis quest. The librarians will urge anybody with those ideas to pick a doctor or find a library with a specialty in current medicine (which turns out to be a very hard task, even in New York City). The library consists of books on all aspects of the history of medicine and health sciences.

The main reading room is a rectangular space with high shelves along each wall, with study space consisting mainly of hardwood tables and chairs. Unlike most libraries, NYAM did not allow me to take any pictures, so the best mental image I can offer is the library of Downton Abbey. The books visible in the reading room are the tip of the iceberg, since the library boasts a collection of more than 500,000 volumes. Their online catalog is run on Koha, an open access system, and they use ByWater as their automation service provider. Searching that catalog, I saw that the books were arranged in Library of Congress order.

From a long-past visit to NYAM, I remember that their most significant holding is a set of George Washington's false teeth, but I was quickly corrected by Shaner that museum holdings of the organization are separate from those of the library. I asked what item they would consider to be their most significant holding, and I was told that it was *de Re Culinaria* by Apicius, a ninth century manuscript written by German monks in Fulda, consisting of recipes from the monastery kitchen. That is their oldest cookbook, but cookery seems to be a major subject at NYAM, since their catalog lists nearly 2000 titles on the subject.

I also asked them who was the most famous person to use their library. The answer came quickly from Shaner, who mentioned Sir William Osler, a famous physician who founded Johns Hopkins Hospital, and author of *The Principles and Practice of Medicine*, a milestone book used in medical education for most of the twentieth century.

Asked about their funding, they told me that the three main factors were the endowments that created the organization in 1847, grants, and an active Friends of the Rare Books Room organization. Memberships begin at $75 for a basic membership and continue up to $10,000 for a Vesalius Circle Benefactor, whose benefits include a cocktail party for the member and 15 of his or her friends.

With a collection this rich in pre-1923 titles, digitization would seem like a natural pursuit. "We have digitized eleven titles, but we are making plans for a much bigger effort in the future," said Garner.

LIBRARY: NEW YORK PUBLIC LIBRARY SCIENCE, INDUSTRY AND BUSINESS LIBRARY

188 Madison Avenue, New York, NY 10016
URL: http://www.nypl.org/locations/sibl
Telephone: (917) 275-6975
Transportation: Bus line M34, M3, or M4; subway: NRQ Herald Square

After visiting the New York Academy of Medicine, a major source of books in the history of medicine, I was interested in locating a library with current information about medicine that would be open to the public. It turns out that this is a task that is nearly impossible. There were far more free law libraries than I could cover in this book, but practically nothing in the way of medicine. There are a number of fine medical libraries in the five boroughs, but they are universally closed to the public. One hospital library in Queens was listed in a directory as being open to the public. When I called them the librarian was evasive about what level of access a citizen might have. When I told her why I wanted to visit her library, evasive turned to hostile as I was told that I may not mention her library in my book. It reminded me of a line in *The Hitchhiker's Guide to the Galaxy*—"We hope we may be able to serve you in some other lifetime."

I turned to the METRO organization in New York City and worked with a librarian who specialized in medical institutions. She encountered the same kind of slammed doors that I had found.

I finally decided that I would settle on a well-funded branch of the New York Public Library (NYPL). I first looked in at the SIBL (Science, Industry and Business Library) on Madison off of 34th Street. This is a beautiful and impressive library, but their selection of medical reference was unremarkable— no more than you might find in a Long Island public library. I had spent a few minutes looking in the catalog to get an idea of which section to visit (SIBL has a combination of Dewey and Library of Congress—the circulating books were Dewey and the reference was Library of Congress), and I noticed that a lot of medical reference titles were found in the Mid-Manhattan library, across 5th Avenue from the main library. I decided to throw my lot in with that library.

LIBRARY: NEW YORK PUBLIC LIBRARY MID-MANHATTAN BRANCH

Address: 455 Fifth Avenue, New York, NY
URL: http://www.nypl.org/locations/mid-manhattan-library

Telephone: (917) 275-6975

E-mail: http://www.questionpoint.org/crs/servlet/org.oclc.admin. BuildForm?&institution=10208&type=1&language=1

Access: Open to the public

Facebook: https://www.facebook.com/midmanhattanlibrary?fref=ts

When I visited on a Friday in the spring, the Mid-Manhattan was bustling in a way that almost approached the crowds on 42nd Street. I found that medical reference was located on the 4th floor, so I headed up the crowded elevator. I soon found the medical reference ranges and they immediately told me a story about what is happening in library reference, at least in the medical sciences. First of all, there was a substantial medical reference collection here—at least 20 full shelves by my count. However, there were a number of empty shelves in the same area. This tells me that the library is moving from paper reference to online at a pretty fast clip. I would guess that these books are being replaced by databases that are accessible only in the library, as opposed to databases that you can access from home using the barcode on your NYPL card. I checked on their Web page and found that this was true for about two-thirds of the 35 medical databases that they listed.

One database that everyone can use is Medline, and in checking up on the Mid-Manhattan branch, I saw that they held programs for people who wanted to get the most out of this comprehensive medical database supplied by the government.

As reference information flows from paper-based to the Cloud, there seems little likelihood that New York City will ever get a truly world-class medical library that can be used by members of the public. In case I am right, the Mid-Manhattan branch of the NYPL seems like the best alternative.

FURTHER READING

Celebrating the contributions of William Osler: http://www.medicalarchives.jhmi.edu/osler/biography.htm.

George Washington didn't have wooden teeth: http://www.smithsonianmag.com/ist/?next=/smart-news/george-washington-didnt-have-wooden-teeth-they-were-ivory-180953273/.

Health links from the Library of Congress: http://www.loc.gov/rr/askalib/virtualref.html#health.

Recommended Health & Medicine titles at New York Public Library: http://www.nypl.org/weblinks/health.

Video about New York Public Library planning to sell the Mid-Manhattan branch: https://www.youtube.com/watch?v=GxWzDRPHSqY.

Yelp review of the NYPL Mid-Manhattan branch: http://www.yelp.com/biz/new-york-public-library-mid-manhattan-library-new-york.

CHAPTER 5

Rare Books

If we encounter a man of rare intellect, we should ask him what books he reads.

Ralph Waldo Emerson

LIBRARY: BERG COLLECTION OF THE NEW YORK PUBLIC LIBRARY

Address: Fifth Avenue at 42nd Street, Third Floor, Room 320, New York, NY 10018
URL: http://www.nypl.org/about/divisions/berg-collection-english-and-american-literature
Telephone: (212) 930-0802
E-mail: berg@nypl.org
Access: Open to researchers by appointment

Before I started this project, I had no idea how many deep specialty collections were lurking behind the lions of the New York Public Library (NYPL). A visit to one of the first libraries netted me a clue that I should look into things like the Pforzheimer Foundation's Shelley and His Circle Collection and the Berg Collection of English and American literature. I held out until close to the end because I wanted access as an author writing a book about special moments that could be had in New York City libraries, but I could never establish a dialog with the one person who could control such access. That led me to plan B. I just used my credentials as a card-carrying NYPL patron (and the fact that Google Scholar shows me as having written more than 70 articles, cited 150 times) and had no trouble arranging a visit.

The excuse for this visit was to see a book that I had actually wanted to see for some time—*All Strange Away*, written by Samuel Beckett, illustrated by Edward Gorey, and signed by both. This was a case of two men whose work I had admired for decades, and it was a surprise to find that they had worked together. Even though the prose is available in reprint, I wanted the experience of reading it for the first time in a room with a very special ambience, surrounded by first editions of Dickens and Thackeray.

In confirming my reservation, the librarian told me that I should pay special attention to the rules for this visit, detailed in great length on a special Website. This page told me that I could not bring in outerwear, a briefcase, or a pen. I could bring in a laptop and a camera. I decided to just go with a smartphone, since it could do the work of both. The Web page also told me that just bearing a valid NYPL card was not enough. I needed a special Berg Collection card to use the collection.

Came the day of my visit, I went to the coat check to leave my coat and my briefcase, but the desk was empty of staff. A nearby security guard told me that the attendant was in the bathroom and should be back soon. Soon turned out to be at least 10 minutes. Then I went up to the third floor to get my special Berg card in Room 318. That room was boarded up for renovations, but I was directed to Room 217 on the second floor, and they would take care of everything. That turned out to be a service desk with one attendant and lots of patrons waiting. Finally I got to the front, where I was told that there was no such thing as a special Berg card. I went back up to the third floor and was eventually let in to the Berg. The rather pleasant young librarian signed me up for the card, and I was ready to see my book. By the time I had filled out the request form and the request form to request a request form, the book was waiting for me, and I sat down to enjoy it.

The book was in a slip case, and I transferred the immaculate copy to a foam wedge book holder. The story began with these words: "Imagination dead imagination. A place, that again. Never another question." The irony was duly noted. Gorey's illustrations were about three inches square— moody, abstract scenes reminiscent of his illustrations in *The West Wing*. I was surprised not to see the autographs on the title page, but it turned out that they were the last thing in the book. Beckett personally inscribed it to the Berg Collection.

A volunteer downstairs had told me that if I asked nicely I could see the collection's flagship holding—the original manuscript of *The Waste Land*. Sadly, that was the one thing they would not let me see. Only the chief librarian could authorize *The Waste Land*, so April truly became the cruelest month.

Next I checked the card catalog for T.E. Lawrence. They had a numbered edition of *The Mint*, but so does my shelf at home. I was really excited to see a listing for the 1926 edition of *Seven Pillars of Wisdom*. This was a subscriber's edition for people in the Downton class, containing full-color illustrations throughout. However, I was quickly told that it was miscataloged. The actual book in the stacks is the 1935 edition that was printed right after Lawrence's death. I checked to see if they have the Kelmscott *Chaucer,* but they do not.

While this was going on, there was a frequent uproar at the glass door to the room. Lots of people would love to go in and check out these treasures, but few of them will take the trouble to make a reservation. Every so often a librarian would go to the door and calmly explain what is needed for eventual access to the room.

I took a good look around the perimeter of the room—glass cases filled with first editions in fine bindings. Also, in the northeast corner of the room you will see Dickens' desk and lamp. Dickens' portable writing desk is also in the glass case on the south wall.

I made sure that the Berg card was good for a year, because I intend to go back and catch up with *The Waste Land.*

LIBRARY: MORGAN LIBRARY

Address: 225 Madison Avenue, New York, NY 10016
URL: http://www.themorgan.org/
Telephone: (212) 685-0008
E-mail: http://www.themorgan.org/research/reading-room-application
Access: Open to researchers by appointment
Facebook: https://www.facebook.com/morganlibrary
Twitter: https://twitter.com/MorganLibrary

When we first moved to New York in 1990, the Morgan Library was high on our list of sites to visit. One day in the early 1990s we made the journey and, arriving at the south entrance, the first thing we saw was a copy of the Gutenberg Bible. That set the tone for the visit, which also included a copy of the signed Declaration of Independence; manuscripts by Mozart, Beethoven, Mark Twain, Steinbeck, and others; topped off by a selection of medieval manuscripts that were visually in the same league as the *Book of Kells.*

Even though I had placed the Morgan on the original list of libraries, I was on the fence about including it as the project wound down. Was it a library with public access to specific research materials or was it a museum about great books and manuscripts? One day when visiting the American

Kennel Club library across the street, I paid it a visit to make sure. I found to my relief that it did have a reading room. Even though I had to justify my visit, it met my criteria for inclusiveness. I was quickly able to contact John Vincler, Director of the Reading Room, and we arranged for a visit several weeks in the future.

To begin a visit to the reading room you must first choose an object or objects that you would like to see. I chose an illustrated edition of *The Rime of the Ancient Mariner* from the mid-nineteenth century. I also chose a manuscript by Mark Twain writing to his publisher with a brief biography of his life that included a very detailed account of how he came upon his pseudonym.

The Morgan library is a fairly easy walk from Penn Station. If the weather had been bad, I could have taken the M4, which loads on 32nd Street outside the station door, and taken a ride right up to the library. Like the special collections of the NYPL, the Morgan has a large set of rules for using the reading room, and like those of its neighbors, the results are well worth it. I was told to use the staff entrance, from which a security guard escorted me to the elevator, which let me off outside the room. I took advantage of storage lockers to eliminate every bit of baggage but the clothes on my back and my cell phone.

The southern entrance to the Morgan Library.

The reading room is a two-story modern facility, with tables on the lower floor and every bit of shelf space taken up with precious volumes. The librarian told me that I may take pictures for my own use (but not publication), but if I did, I must include a strip of paper in each shot identifying the work as an item in the Morgan collection. The photographer in me had to take a back seat to the writer in this case.

The next item really gave me chills. It was a manuscript letter by Mark Twain. It begins oddly enough in the third person and then slips into the first person about the time he is describing his first trip west. He explicitly describes how he took the name from an old steamboat captain who used it for writing humorous bits about the river. The old man died shortly after Clemens moved west and, he writes, "The body was not cold in the ground before I took that name."

Now I was met by John Vincler, a surprisingly young director of the reading room. At my age (let us just say that I remember when Truman was President), many people look young, but he appeared to be in his mid-thirties. He began by taking me down to the heart of the enterprise— J.P. Morgan's personal library. The room faces Madison Avenue, and it is dark—probably deliberately so to prevent fading of the spines of the very precious volumes. "A few shelves near his desk can be turned to reveal their true contents—art books from the centuries past."

A room to the side looks into a large stack area, filled with the best of the best items. As I looked through the rows of leather-bound volumes, I saw a riveting sight—something that looked like a baseball in a glass cube. The founder of my bank was known to play hardball with the best of them, but was he a Yankees fan? It turns out that the object was a tiny world globe.

Walking out and just down the hall there is a room that is used for special displays, but Vincler was quick to point out that this room has some very special history. It was the office of Belle da Costa Greene, a mixed-race woman hired by Morgan to be his private librarian. She was famous for her comptence and her devotion to Morgan. Among her other after-work accomplishments, Vincler told me that she was said to be the lover of Bernard Berenson. He said that there is quite a bit of information about Greene and the Morgan in general in the book *The Making of the Morgan*.

Next we went into the main reading room, which is the showcase for the public displays of their greatest treasures. Again, there was a Gutenberg Bible on display. "We actually have three of them," said Vincler. As in the reading room, there is a second story with more books, but no visible way of getting to them. Vincler tugs at a shelf near the door and it swivels open to reveal a secret stairway leading up.

During the visits to libraries for this project I would see many amazing things, but it is hard to top the Morgan for your basic "wow factor." I speculated that this young man must wake up mornings in sheer disbelief that he gets to do this for a living. At the end, as I was getting back to the locker to retrieve my bag, I happened to mention that one library had a card catalog showing that they owned the precious 1926 privately printed version of *Seven Pillars of Wisdom*, but that turned out to be a mistake. They really had the 1935 version, which is also on my shelf at home. Vincler looked it up and confirmed that they really do have the 1926. I am compiling a list of things to do after I finish this book. The Morgan Library is high on that list.

FURTHER READING

Article about John Vincler: http://www.finebooksmagazine.com/fine_books_blog/2014/06/bright-young-librarians-john-vincler.phtml.

Google Books preview of Making of the Morgan by Paul Spencer Byard: https://books.google.com/books?id=5BAsyC6tA78C&lpg=PA26&dq=belle%20da%20costa%20morgan&pg=PA26#v=onepage&q=belle%20da%20costa%20morgan&f=false.

Kelmscott Chaucer online: http://www.rarebookroom.org/Control/chkwks/index.html.

Page containing an illustration from Lawrence's subscirber's edition: http://www.hrc.utexas.edu/collections/books/holdings/telawrence/.

Review of Beckett/Gorey's All Strange Away: http://www.english.fsu.edu/jobs/num05/Num5murphy.htm.

Rime of the Ancient Mariner: http://nzr.mvnu.edu/faculty/trearick/english/rearick/readings/works/lyric_po/rime.htm.

University of Virginia page about the Waste Land: http://people.virginia.edu/~sfr/enam312/tsehp.html.

CHAPTER 6

Art

When I was a child my mother said to me, 'If you become a soldier, you'll be a general. If you become a monk, you'll be the pope.' Instead I became a painter and wound up as Picasso.

Pablo Picasso

LIBRARY: MUSEUM OF MODERN ART

Address: 11 West 53rd Street, New York, NY 10019
URL: http://www.moma.org/learn/resources/library/index
Telephone: (212) 708-9433
E-mail: http://www.moma.org/about/info/
Access: For researchers by advance appointment
Facebook: https://www.facebook.com/MuseumofModernArt?fref=photo
Twitter: https://twitter.com/MoMALibrary

I cannot remember the first time I visited the Museum of Modern Art (MOMA), but it must have been in the early 1990s when we first moved east. We have stayed with them over the years—even visiting the temporary MOMA in Queens when the Midtown building was undergoing renovation. We have joined the museum several times over the years, including the past year, so I was particularly eager to visit this library. When I first e-mailed the library, there was a prompt response from the reference librarian, and an appointment was set up.

The restrictions for visitors on their Web page sound a bit draconian, but when I got there, I found everyone to be pleasant and helpful. I did have to leave most of my gear in a locker, but once I did that, and got my elevator pass, everything went like clockwork.

50 Specialty Libraries of New York City
ISBN 978-0-08-100554-5

Display area overlooking 54th Street.

The library overlooks the sculpture garden and the main floors of the museum. I checked in with Jennifer, the reference librarian, who suggested that I look around, and told me it was alright to take pictures, as long as I did not take a recognizable picture of any of the library users. I mentioned to her that the restrictions on the Web page made it sound tougher than it really was, and she admitted that maybe they could revisit that. The ready reference shelf was in Library of Congress order, and it included bound volumes of the Museum's journal. This was followed by shelves of volumes related to past MOMA exhibitions, which seemed to be in chronological order.

Current journals reading area.

Minutes later, the library director Milan Hughston came around the corner and invited me into his office for a brief interview. It turned out that we had Long Island in common, since he owns a home on the east end of the island, just short of the Hamptons. He told me that the library owns over 300,000 books. The items he is most proud of are the artists' ephemera. These are collections pertaining to MOMA exhibitions, including objects such as announcement cards, press clippings, posters, and flyers. Hughston said that books have been written about this collection.

When asked about famous people who had used the library, he thought for a moment and mentioned that the actress Clare Danes had been in doing research. Funding for the library comes directly from the parent institution.

LIBRARY: FRICK ART REFERENCE LIBRARY

Address: 10 East 71st Street, New York, NY 10021
URL: http://www.frick.org/research/library
Telephone: (212) 547-0641
E-mail: library@frick.org
Access: Open to the public
Twitter: https://twitter.com/fricklibrary

The Frick Collection is, I will admit, one of the few museums on the Upper East Side that I had never visited. I was not even entirely clear on the matter of what set them apart from other museums on 5th Avenue. Several other librarians I had interviewed asked me something like "You're doing the Frick, aren't you?" That was an easy answer because they were always on my target list, and it got even easier when I made my first call to the library, and I was quickly forwarded to Heidi Rosenau, Associate Director of Media Relations & Marketing. Heidi was quite enthused about being in the book and quickly set up a meeting with the highly distinguished people who managed the library.

The meeting was arranged with Heidi; Stephen Bury, the Andrew Mellon Chief Librarian; and Inge Reist, Director of the Center for the History of Collecting, an initiative within the library. Among other activities, the Center works with the Pennsylvania State University Press for the publication of scholarly works. We sat in an office just off the main reading room, and the three Frick administrators filled me in on the museum and library's story.

This library is just short of its hundredth anniversary, as it was founded by Helen Clay Frick, as a memorial to her father, Henry Clay Frick, an industrialist and avid art collector, in 1920. He was interested in knowing more about the artists whose works filled his house, and Helen took up that cause with energy, determination, and note cards. The library in the early days shared a space with the bowling alley in the basement of the Frick mansion and finally moved into its current quarters in 1935.

In the beginning, she had been inspired by the work of English Scholar Robert Witt, who had amassed a large library of photographic images of paintings. I was told that this collection included 1.25 million images. A large number of these works are found in private collections, but Miss Frick was able to use her high society connections to open a number of mansion doors to the photographers.

This has a number of uses. My guides pointed out to me that even paintings by the masters can be altered to suit the artistic tastes of the time when they show up for auction. To prove it they showed me several images of the same painting from which a face in the original went missing. Also, the collection had a use that Miss Frick may not have anticipated at the time. During World War II, the collection was closed for six months while the government used its data to pinpoint the location of rare art and smooth the transition to repatriation. As part of this effort, the museum produced 700 maps to show allied pilots where to avoid bombing campaigns.

Art book with documentation.

In addition to a major collection of books in art reference, the Frick also owns thousands of art auction catalogs, as well as pamphlets from dealers.

When asked about famous users of the library, I was told that everyone in art criticism has walked through these doors at some time or another. Also, it was mentioned that Jackson Pollock had been to the library.

The library has more than 200,000 books in total, but there is more to its bragging rights. They ran a survey in WorldCat and found that 27% of the books in their collection were not found in the massive bibliographic database—meaning that these books are unique holdings in the library world. Among the more significant holdings here are a 1727 catalog of the Duke D'Orléans. They are very proud of their manuscript of the Cavendish Square Art Collection. Holdings are described in an Innovative Interfaces catalog or enhanced in a Primo discovery system. The books are all reference, even for museum members, and they are arranged in Library of Congress order.

Fine art book from the collection.

After our talk, we took a brief tour of the library facility. As we went through the reading room, we had to hold our voices down, because nearly every seat was taken by with someone in deep research. Upstairs, I was shown the original office of Helen Frick—left more or less the way it was with the exception of a computer at the desk. From what I had been hearing of Frick, she would have certainly approved, because she proved to be a proponent of using the latest technology at all times.

Book restoration desk.

Upper floors included an in-house facility for the restoration of books, as well as a state-of-the-art digitization facility.

Digitization room.

Next, they took me to the penthouse floor, where we walked out into a magnificent view of Central Park and west to the Hudson River.

Looking west towards the park.

For a final surprise, Ms Rosenau took me on a quick tour of the art museum. Arguably the most famous holding is the portrait of Thomas More by Hans Holbein. One might consider this the equivalent of MOMA's *Starry Night*, but unlike the Van Gogh painting, it was easy to stand in front of More without being jostled by crowds of people taking selfies with the great work. Rosenau feels that Bellini's *St. Francis in the Desert* is the key holding of the collection.

The Frick Collection Library is an outstanding resource for anyone interested in researching in-depth material about the art of Western Civilization.

LIBRARY: COOPER HEWITT

Address: 2 East 91st Street
URL: http://library.si.edu/libraries/cooper-hewitt-smithsonian-design-library
Telephone: (212) 849-8400
Access: Open to the public

Facebook: https://www.facebook.com/cooperhewitt?fref=nf
Transportation: Bus line M3 or M4

When we were newly minted New Yorkers, fresh off the boat from Arizona, we visited the Cooper Hewitt Museum early in our stay. I only knew that it was a Smithsonian museum and that the focus was more on the practical side of artistry. I had not seen the library at the time, so I was very pleased to find out that they kept a library that was well within the bounds of this project, being open to the public. I set up an interview with the library director, Stephen Van Dyk. I found out that it is possible to walk to this library from 70th Street, but not in 15 minutes.

Library reference area.

While waiting for Stephen, I took my own quick tour of the library and found it to be humming with activity.

Stephen met me in a rather magnificent meeting room to the side of the library, filled with reference books and dark wood paneling. He explained that the Cooper Hewitt was an outgrowth of the Cooper Union facility in Greenwich Village, founded in 1896 at the behest of three granddaughters of Peter Cooper—Sarah Cooper Hewitt, Eleanor Garnier Hewitt, and Amy

Hewitt Green. The museum was stationed on the fourth floor of the school building, and it provided information about decorative arts, as well as a library for people who had no other access. The mission of the museum was to provide practical art for working designers.

Shelves in the library's research area.

The library began to collect manuals from institutions such as the Victoria and Albert Museum. As part of their museum work, they collected hundreds of thousands of images. They started a school for women designers, and after the death of the founders, the museum pioneered the idea of the museum gift shop.

Over time, the museum and the school went on divergent paths, and in 1963, it was announced that the Cooper Union would shut down the museum. There was a tremendous outcry from the public, leading to the rescue of the museum by the Smithsonian, reopening uptown in a house that was originally the home of Andrew Carnegie. After considerable planning, the new museum mounted its first exhibition in 1974.

The museum then forged a partnership with the Parsons School of Design. They currently maintain a graduate program with 100 students. Van Dyk often takes time out from his library duties to act as a thesis advisor for these students.

Examples of the library's collection of fine bindings.

I asked Stephen if he could name any famous people who had used the library. He mentioned that Martin Scorsese had used the library to help get an authentic look for the film *The Age of Innocence*.

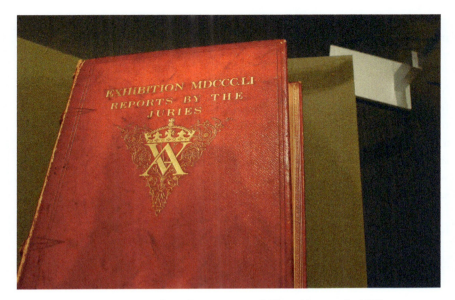

Exhibition report from the Victoria and Albert Museum in 1851.

I soon picked up on the fact that Van Dyk's great passion here was in fine bindings. He mentioned the name of a London binder that made a special binding of only 2 copies. One of them went down on the Titanic. The other was at this library. His proudest holding is a book published by the Victoria and Albert Museum in 1851 in honor of their juried exhibition.

LIBRARY: WHITNEY MUSEUM OF AMERICAN ART–FRANCES MULHALL ACHILLES LIBRARY

Address: 610 West 26th Street
URL: http://whitney.org/Research/Library
Telephone: (212) 570-3682
E-mail: library@whitney.org.
Access: Open to researchers with advance appointment
Facebook: https://www.facebook.com/whitneymuseum?fref=ts
Twitter: https://twitter.com/whitneymuseum
Transportation: Subway: C&E line to 23rd Street

I had not been to the Whitney since sometime in the 1990s at their previous Midtown location, so I was very happy to revisit them at a time of exciting change. When I first contacted librarian Ivy Blackman about a visit in support of the book, I was gratified to get a quick response. We set up a visit on a Friday morning on a beautiful spring day.

I arrived at Penn Station an hour before the appointment, and I could have saved some leg work by taking the subway to 23rd Street, but I decided to just make the walk. It was at least a half-hour, and when I got there, I had to double check the address, which bore no sign of housing a library. It was a medium tall building in an industrial area near the High Line. Scrolling through the buzzer list, I finally did see Library, so I pushed the button and was quickly told by Ivy that I could go up to the eighth floor. Walking in, I saw a stairway to my right, and no sign of an elevator, so I went ahead. I am nearly 70 and not in the best of shape, so I was very glad to make the last few steps.

Minutes later, Ivy came out and apologized, because there really was an elevator. She led me to the library, stopping in the kitchen to get me a drink of water. We sat down at one of the comfortable library tables and talked about the institution, The library had been there since 2011, and it is assumed that it is its permanent home. Blackman said that the building shared space with the museum's archival and art storage. The library holds 70,000 volumes, of which 10% are in special collections. They index their collection on a Voyager catalog, which came online in 2000.

The books are arranged in Library of Congress order. In addition to books, the library also collects posters and graphics.

The museum was founded in the 1920s by Gertrude Vanderbilt Whitney, who had amassed a large collection of American art. She offered the collection to the Metropolitan Museum, but the gift was declined, so she set about to create her own museum. Her collection of books also became the starting point for the Whitney's library.

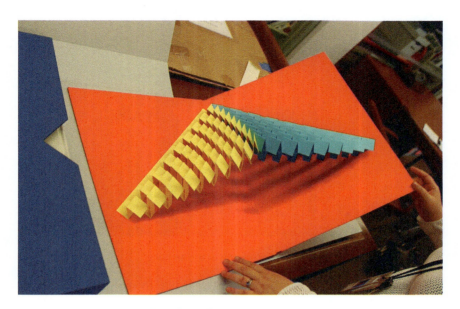

Auerbach's 3 dimensional book.

Blackman pointed to a book by Tauba Auerbach as their flagship holding. She pulled the large book from its case and opened the first page, using the care that you would employ in opening the fingers of a one-day-old infant. It turned out to be a graphic in the shape of a pyramid that unfolds as the book is spread. It is a pop-up book for adults, and each entry was more beautiful than the one before. I was also shown a giant book containing an illustrated short story by Stephen King and privately published by the museum's adjunct operation, the Library Fellows. I asked about digitization, and I was told that they have an active program and that they work with archive.org. I am a long-running fan of archive.org, so I was impressed.

The rare books archive containing these gems also has a collection on artists who have not become household names just yet. At the entrance there is a large range of file cabinets entirely devoted to Edward Hopper. "We like to think of ourselves as an artists' museum, not just a museum of art," Ivy said. To that end, everybody who was anybody in American contemporary art has visited the museum, but the most famous recent visitor was Michelle Obama.

The Hopper section of the archive.

Afterward, Blackman asked me if I would like to see the other library farther downtown at the Whitney's new home at the bottom of the High Line. I told her that I most certainly would, so we headed down on the street and then the High Line. When we got to the museum, we saw that there was a line a block long to get in. I felt very privileged to be going in the staff entrance. When we got off the elevator, I was shown a glass case with a circus scene of small objects designed by Alexander Calder. As we were walking around the corner to see the library I could not help but notice the iconic painting of a cow's skull by Georgia O'Keeffe.

View from the museum library reading room.

The library reading room had a generous meeting area on the ground floor, and there was a stairway up to the book stacks. The reading room is almost entirely for purposes of the museum staff. The west wall was entirely a glass window with a magnificent view of the Hudson River, with a constant show of helicopters ascending. I thanked Ivy for going far beyond the normal hospitality and giving me a total Whitney experience. I have a cache of writing money that I use for museum memberships and Broadway performances, and I am likely to make the Whitney part of my repertoire and avoid that line around the block when I bring my wife.

Files on a considerable number of American artists.

INTERNATIONAL CENTER FOR PHOTOGRAPHY LIBRARY

Address: 1114 Avenue of the Americas at 43rd Street, New York, NY 10036
URL: http://www.icp.org/research-center/library
Telephone: (212) 857-0004
E-mail: library@icp.org
Access: By appointment only
Facebook: https://www.facebook.com/internationalcenterofphotography
Twitter: https://twitter.com/icphotog

My career in photography began in high school in 1961. I was a sickly boy, and missed physical education class more than the coach liked. I should have gone to the nurse's office every time, but I did not, so I failed PE. By the time of my senior year, I was short a half credit, so I took photography class instead of study hall. It was absolutely the best class I ever took in high school, and I took the second semester even though I did not need the credit. I also learned a lot from my father, whose pictures of the Philippines have been posted on the Web and enjoyed by thousands. He taught me one very important lesson—when taking pictures of people, get right up into their faces.

I had to look twice at the address, because what you see of the International Center for Photography from 6th Avenue looks about as big as a Taco Bell. After that it is not hard to figure out that 97% of the institution is underground.

I found the library easily enough. It was in a compact space with every possible foot of shelf space containing books and periodicals. I was met by Deirdre Donohue, whose official title is Stephanie Shuman Librarian. She told me that the current building was constructed in 2001, but the school has been in existence since 1974. She told me that hers is one of two funded chairs at the school. This is a very stable position, as she is only the fourth librarian in the past 40 years. It is unusual for a college in that the library is open to the public with a minimum of restrictions, although advance reservations do need to be made.

When I asked which famous people had been in to use the library, there was a good selection, given that HBO headquarters is right next door. Names that came up included Gabriel Byrne and Diane Keaton. The library is reference only, although students in the Master's program can take books back to their studios.

In one side of the room there is an appealing space for journals. Their Web page lists 44 journals on their subscription list. Their Web-based online catalog is provided by a company out of California named Libraryworld, and their 25,000 holdings are noted in OCLC. They are arranged on the shelves in Library of Congress order. New books are often provided as gifts from alumni and publishers. There is an annual book sale that helps with the outright purchase of new acquisitions. When I asked which book they consider to be their flagship holding, I was quickly shown the title *The Decisive Moment* by Henri Cartier-Bresson. It has a long inscription on the title page from the author to one of the school's founders.

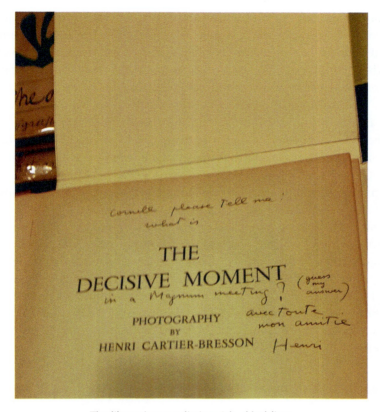

The library's most distinguished holding.

There is a substantial program in digitization, although most of it is for the internal use of the school. Deirdre told me that they are particularly interested in making high-definition images of book covers. They did 100 as a test case, and the file sizes were astronomical—going into the terabytes of data. This is one of those libraries that I hope to revisit someday when I can look in as an interested amateur photographer rather than an author.

LIBRARY: THE REANIMATION LIBRARY

Address: 543 Union Street, Brooklyn, NY 11215
URL: http://www.reanimationlibrary.org/pages/about
Facebook: https://www.facebook.com/reanimationlibrary
Twitter: https://twitter.com/reanimationlib

This library was not on my list until another librarian in an art library mentioned it and thought it would be very appropriate for the book. It turned out that she was absolutely right. There is a lot of talk these days that the whole concept of a library is obsolete and that we will be swept off the edge of the planet by waves of unfiltered information on the Internet. This library makes one of the better cases for the ways in which libraries can adapt and thrive in a revolutionary environment.

The library exists in a cluster of artistic enterprises at a location in the Gowanus section of Brooklyn that you might describe as "off the beaten path." On the relatively short walk from the subway to the building, I saw signs that this part of the city was ripe for a revival—starting with trendy ice cream shops and authentic-looking barbeque eateries.

I rang the buzzer and was soon greeted by Andrew Beccone, the visionary who is creating a second life for illustrated books that he finds at garage sales and thrift shops. "These books were left for dead, but this library is breathing new life into them." The library is tiny compared to most I have visited. Beccone has been collecting books since 2001, and the library concept came along a few years later. Along the way he got his library degree from Pratt (like almost everyone else I visited in Brooklyn).

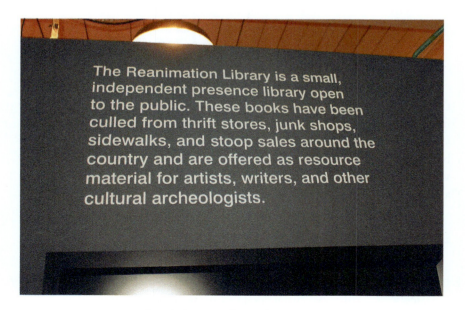

The Reanimation Library is a small, independent presence library open to the public. These books have been culled from thrift stores, junk shops, sidewalks, and stoop sales around the country and are offered as resource material for artists, writers, and other cultural archeologists.

Inscription over the reading room.

The rules seem clear. No juvenile books, no arty books. Practical books that show the underlying structure of moving things. The library is totally self-funded. Books may not be checked out, but Beccone encourages people to make images in-house and send them out through the Internet. Famous visitors include Jonathan Lethem, author of *Chronic City*, and many artists. "I think of this room as my studio and the library is a work of art."

The small but powerful library.

He is not the only one who holds that opinion. At one time he moved the entire library of 2000+ books across the river and it sat as an exhibit for several weeks at the Museum of Modern Art. He has also been sent to places as far away as Beirut to create similar projects in other countries, using materials that he can find in their book stores and thrift shops.

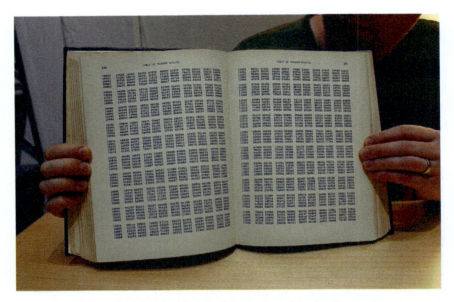

In Beccone's hands, a book of random numbers becomes art.

I asked what he considered to be his most significant holding. He reached into the psychology shelves and pulled out a book called *The Behavior of Man*. Some bell rang in the back of my head. I have seen this book before. It was my textbook at Phoenix College for Psychology 101, exactly 50 years ago. The synchronicity dial was off the grid at this point.

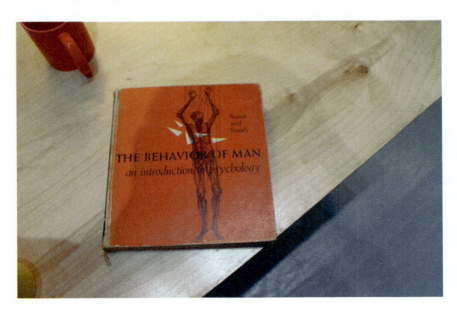

Andrew's favorite book and my psychology text from college.

Andrew is also fascinated with the concept of the online catalog. He agreed with me that the problem with online catalogs is that they still operate under the paradigm of the catalog card—a MARC record is just a computer format for the information on a catalog card. He found a way to create a custom-designed online catalog, including images in the records. Do not tell anyone, but he could get rich pursuing this idea in a field that is ripe for change.

I must admit that this visit was one of the biggest surprises in my travels for this book. Beccone has taken the concept of a library, put his own spin on it, and made it work beautifully. I found this to be inspiring.

FURTHER READING

Artists' ephemera from MOMA: https://www.moma.org/visit/calendar/exhibitions/1377.

Blog about the history of the Hewitt Sisters: http://library.si.edu/libraries/cooper-hewitt/hewitt-sisters.

Details about the Thomas More painting: http://collections.frick.org/view/objects/asitem/items$0040:100.

Exploring the Museum of Modern Art Library: http://www.libraryasincubatorproject.org/?p=14086.

Internet Movie Database article on Age of Innocence: http://www.imdb.com/title/tt0106226/?ref_=nv_sr_1.

MOMA article about Milan Hughston: http://post.at.moma.org/profiles/446-milan-hughston.

New York Heritage Digitization project with the Whitney Library 1907-1930: http://cdm16694.contentdm.oclc.org/cdm/landingpage/collection/p15405coll1.

New York Times Laud's Cooper Hewitt's Object of the day blog: http://www.bates.edu/news/2013/01/18/new-york-times-cooper-hewitt-object-of-the-day-blog-baumann-87/.

Observer article about the Frick, focusing on Inge Reist: http://observer.com/2009/11/at-the-frick-a-focus-on-the-collector-as-art-history/.

Sangorski and Sutcliffe article: https://en.wikipedia.org/wiki/Sangorski_%26_Sutcliffe.

Whitney collection at Archive.org: https://archive.org/details/whitneymuseum&tab=about.

Wikipedia entry for Stephen Bury: https://en.wikipedia.org/wiki/Stephen_J._Bury.

CHAPTER 7

Psychology

Show me a sane man and I'll cure him for you.

Carl Gustav Jung

THE KRISTINE MANN LIBRARY

URL: http://01772fa.netsolhost.com/visitthelibrary.html

Telephone: (212) 697-7877

E-mail: info@junglibrary.org

Facebook: https://www.facebook.com/pages/Kristine-Mann-Library/
48833244389?fref=ts

Online Catalog: http://catalog.nycjung.bywatersolutions.com/cgi-bin/
koha/opac-main.pl

The Kristine Mann Library is devoted to the study of Carl Gustav Jung (1875–1961), a Swiss psychologist who, early in his career, became a favored protégé of Sigmund Freud. The two men had a major falling out, substantially over Freud's insistence that libido is the most important factor in human behavior. Jung went on to found his own school, which, like Freud, paid attention to dream interpretation. The library's namesake, Kristine Mann (1873–1945), was a psychiatrist who studied under Jung in the early 1920s and later went on to become one of the cofounders of the Analytical Psychology Club of New York. At her death in 1945, she willed her collection to the group, founding the current library, which has been housed at its current location for about 30 years.

50 Specialty Libraries of New York City
ISBN 978-0-08-100554-5

Entrance to library.

The library is divided into two smallish rooms. The south room, which one enters first, contains the service desk, stacks of books, and a number of Jung-inspired paintings, as well as the card catalog, which has been generally supplanted by an online catalog. A curtain separates this room from the west room, which contains more books, considerable sculpture, and the copy machine. In a visit late on a Thursday night, the west room was generating the most activity. Just before closing time, there were several users, who seemed to be graduate students, in earnest contemplation, while the copy machine was in constant use.

Research room.

The assistant librarian supplied some of the basic facts. The Kristine Mann library has been in existence since 1945 and at its current Midtown location since 1980. The collection contains about 10,000 titles. Anyone can come in to use the collection, but to borrow books you must join the library for a $50 annual fee. He stressed that the collection included a considerable number of titles in subjects that Jung considered to be important, such as Eastern religions, mythology, and dream interpretation.

I noticed that the arrangement of the books seemed to be following some sort of homemade system with categories such as Asia or Dream. It was confirmed that this is the case.

The librarian also said that it is hard to pin down the average user of the library, although authors and students were a major factor. Also, he pointed out that the library is affiliated with the New York Jung Center, which brings in numbers of prospective Jungian analysts who are interested in the library's resources.

LIBRARY: AMERICAN SOCIETY FOR PSYCHICAL RESEARCH

Address: 5 West 73rd Street
URL: http://www.aspr.com/
Telephone: (212) 799-5050
E-mail: aspr@aspr.com
Access: Open to researchers by advanced appointment
Facebook: https://www.facebook.com/pages/American-Society-for-Psychical-Research/108396505855130
Transportation: Subway B&C line, 72nd Street

Sometimes I got my best leads on libraries to visit from other libraries I visited. Such was the case with the American Society for Psychical Research (ASPR), which was recommended to me by two other librarians in very different types of libraries. After a series of e-mail correspondences, I settled on April 1, 2015. This was significant because it was the only day on which I visited four libraries in Manhattan. The main thing I learned from that experience was to visit no more than three libraries on a given day. However, the staff there could not have been more welcoming, so I counted the visit as a success.

The society is in a well-kept old mansion just west of Central Park and across the street from a subway stop. The staff noticed that I looked a bit tired, so they sat me down in a comfortable chair and brought out a bottle of water. Patrice Keane, the society director, was stuck in traffic on the 59th Street Bridge and phoned in to apologize. She asked that her intern begin the process of showing me around the archive until she could make it over to the West Side.

Library decor on the second floor.

The intern showed me the archive area, and one of the areas there struck me as totally unique. "This is the sensory deprivation room," she announced. It reminded me of the darkrooms we used to use back in the day when students developed film, but it seemed just large enough for a person to sit down at a small desk. The point was to block out all conflicting sensory data when an ESP test was being run. The intern admitted that the tests had not been run for a few years, but they had plans to continue soon. She also showed me a large section of shelves containing spirit photography books. She admitted that a good number of the photographs were probably fake, but they were interesting as art.

Main reading room.

Finally we went to the reading room—four walls of ceiling-high shelves with a window overlooking 73rd Street. As I glanced to the left, I immediately recognized a book that is also on my shelf—the extraordinary *The Tao of Physics* by Fritjof Capra, which attempts to find common ground in Eastern religions and quantum physics. Since it is a known fact that human observation can change the behavior of subatomic particles, it is a compelling concept, but lots of scientists scoff at the notion.

Soon Ms. Keane arrived, somewhat frazzled by the drive, but ready to talk. She told me that the facility has approximately 20,000 volumes, and the thing that makes them proudest is the complete archive of the *Journal of the American Society for Psychical Research*. She is very proud of her organization, which was founded by William James and Harry Houdini, among others. They have an active program of working with nearby colleges and universities providing interns. She is also proud of the work that they had been doing in partnership with the Shakers, whose mystical visions were a source of study for the group. They also have a grant funded by the National Institute of Mental Health to study dreams.

Entrance to archive area.

The library has been given 300 boxes of papers from the estate of Montague Ullman, a significant psychologist, and past president of the ASPR. A poster displaying his obituary was found in the group's lobby.

"This is a place for serious research, and visits are only allowed by advance reservation," said Keane. She asked me if all of the specialty libraries had that kind of restriction, but actually I have found that it is about half and half.

One of my standard questions is to find out which famous people had used the library. At first she mentioned that when Ghostbusters came out, Dan Aykroyd had recommended the library to anyone with a serious interest in the supernatural. Then, as I was leaving, she opened up and admitted that many years ago, John and Yoko had come by from their home around the corner. "Stop the presses," I replied.

FURTHER READING

Wikipedia biography of Montague Ullman: http://en.wikipedia.org/wiki/Montague_Ullman.
Carl Jung Home Page: http://www.cgjungpage.org/.

Carl Jung resources for Home Study: http://www.carl-jung.net/.

Description of Shaker Visionary experiences documented by the ASPR: https://books.
google.com/books?id=q8aX4_S47XoC&pg=PR7&lpg=PR7&dq=aspr+shaker&
source=bl&ots=ND6iMZE4pU&sig=BWBB3pArFBlUl32erX1FiKIUqOE&hl=en&sa=
X&ei=18NGVbrFI4e9yQTrzICQCg&ved=0CEoQ6AEwCTgK#v=onepage&q=
aspr%20shaker&f=false.

Jung's theory of dreams: http://members.core.com/~ascensus/docs/jung1.html.

Out of Body experience video: https://www.youtube.com/watch?v=GbkQ2HxYsOM.

Wikipedia biography of Montague Ullman: http://en.wikipedia.org/wiki/Montague_
Ullman.

William James Society: http://wjsociety.org/.

Out of Body experience video: https://www.youtube.com/watch?v=GbkQ2HxYsOM.

Description of Shaker Visionary experiences documented by the ASPR: https://books.
google.com/books?id=q8aX4_S47XoC&pg=PR7&lpg=PR7&dq=aspr+shaker&sour
ce=bl&ots=ND6iMZE4pU&sig=BWBB3pArFBlUl32erX1FiKIUqOE&hl=en&sa=
X&ei=18NGVbrFI4e9yQTrzICQCg&ved=0CEoQ6AEwCTgK#v=onepage&q=
aspr%20shaker&f=false.

William James Society: http://wjsociety.org/.

Out of Body experience video: https://www.youtube.com/watch?v=GbkQ2HxYsOM.

CHAPTER 8

Government Libraries

There are not many who know of its existence, and few who have heard of it know of its location.

New York Times (1898)

LIBRARY: THE MUNICIPAL LIBRARY

Address: 31 Chambers Street, Room 112, New York City, NY 10007
URL: www.nyc.gov/html/records/html/about/chlibrary.shtml
Transportation: Subway A&C line Chambers Street

I rode from Penn Station to the Chambers Street station on the A line and walked east on Chambers Street for about two blocks to find the library. I spoke with Christene Bruzzese (pronounced Brew Zi Si), the supervising librarian. The library is one of the agencies housed in a dark, ornate marble building dating back to the early twentieth century, across the street from the City Hall complex. Walking into the library, my first impression was that the facility is bright and inviting. There is a reading area with comfortable leather chairs next to a fireplace that reminds me of some of the lush university alumni houses that you see uptown, such as the Yale Club or the Princeton Club. There are a number of glass display cases, highlighting useful books and manuscripts.

50 Specialty Libraries of New York City
ISBN 978-0-08-100554-5

Reading area.

Bruzzese said that the library has a collection of 400,000 books and pamphlets. The prevailing holdings are publications of city agencies—some of them dating back to the 1600s. This includes police department reports as far back as 1860 and fire department reports going back to 1850.

Display area in East room of the library.

"Typical users here are authors, students, and city researchers," Bruzzese said. This morning, there were a number of people who would have used the New York State Unified Court System Library, a few blocks up Centre Street, but that library had been closed for renovations for a few weeks. The court system library had printed out flyers that recommended substitute libraries, and City Hall Library was at the head of the list. I had asked about genealogy researchers, but was told that those records were kept in the Municipal Archives, a few doors down.

In the 11 years that Bruzzese had been working at City Hall, the most famous visitor was Mayor Bloomberg, who was in the library to shoot a video. She also mentioned helping Deputy Mayor Cas Holloway and a team of people from the Rudolph Giuliani campaign.

I asked her what was the most unique or valuable item in their collection. She told me that the Common Council minutes dating back to the 1700s would be the most likely answer. "We even have council minutes dating back to the Dutch period." I asked if these were the original handwritten books, but was told that they are printed transcriptions. However, in their display cases you will see centuries-old manuscripts that are owned by the Department of Records–Municipal Archives.

Bruzzese said that the two departments work very closely together.

The library is arranged in three large and equal-sized rooms. You enter into the central room, which houses the service desks, an extensive map collection, and a ready reference area. This room contains the journal and newspaper reading area. Otherwise, it is filled with ranges of books and pamphlets. The nongovernment books are arranged in Dewey order. City and state volumes are given their own classification scheme, loosely based on Library of Congress classification.

The east room contains a substantial number of bound volumes and pamphlets. There is a substantial biography binder collection that includes mainly newspaper clippings of famous New Yorkers. Checking the Ro volume, there was no reference to former police commissioner Theodore Roosevelt, but it did have obituaries, including one for Eleanor Roosevelt, so the project seems to date back to the early 1960s. Each mayor has their own binder, and Robert Moses has a series of them. There are also more display cases with visually appealing items from the library's collection.

The west wing is a new addition to the library—a visitors' center that features items given to the various mayors of New York over time. If the main room of the library is bright and inviting, the visitors' center positively glows. It also contains a gift shop and a collection of crime scene photographs, often featuring mob hits lying in the streets of Brooklyn. One of the more poignant displays is a flag recovered from the ruins of the World Trade Center in 2001.

World Trade Center flag.

A separate room celebrates the long history of the WNYC radio and television station. Devices such as a large reel-to-reel tape deck may need further explanation for younger visitors. The library maintains a collection of all the shows ever produced for the station.

After taking my leave of the City Hall Library, I went to the Municipal Archives. I will admit to being intimidated by microfilm machines, but theirs were some of the most intuitive I have seen. The staff members here are quite knowledgeable and beyond helpful. One of them showed me how to go from a computerized index to the actual birth and marriage records on microfilm. I was on my case within minutes.

Before leaving I spoke with Kenneth R. Cobb, Assistant Commissioner of the New York City Department of Records & Information Services, who is justifiably proud of the work that goes on here.

LIBRARY: NATIONAL ARCHIVES AT NEW YORK CITY

Address: 1 Bowling Green, New York, NY 10004
URL: archive.gov

Telephone: (212) 401–1620
E–mail: newyork.archives@nara.gov
Access: Open to the public
Transportation: Subway line 4 or 5 Bowling Green Station

I had been to this library some 10 years ago when it was on Varick Street in Greenwich Village. At that time, it was a bustling genealogical library where I looked through ships' passenger lists in search of my great grand-mother. Now it is in the Customs House Building along with the Smithsonian Museum of the American Indian. I am told that it was moved south in 2013, right after the Hurricane Sandy disaster. The library's function appears to have been trimmed back to being substantially a repository of government files and court records. Its Web page does list the genealogical component, however, so you would be advised to come see for yourself if possible. When you walk in you are greeted with a striking logo for the archive, as well as giant maps of New York. The exterior of the Customs House did not show any mention of the archive at the time I was there, but I was told that this would be fixed soon.

Main entrance to the National Archive in Lower Manhattan.

Bowling Green is the oldest section of New York City—the location where a mob tore down the statue of King George. It is said that the pillars surrounding the park are the oldest standing structures in the city. The library's north window gives a view down to Bowling Green, and that could hardly be more perfect. When I arrived I had a special mission. Weeks before, I had filled out their online form, explaining what I was doing and asking to speak to someone when I came to visit. When I arrived, I mentioned this to the reference librarian, who seemed slightly horrified. However, she was a good sport and began answering my questions. Further, she called the library director, who agreed to come out in a few minutes and talk to me. I had only hoped to schedule a future meeting, so I was quite pleased to chalk this up in one visit.

It was a slow day, but I have seen this library when it was swamped, so I know what can happen here. I asked which holding they considered to be their most valuable. I got the same answer from both librarians—a copy of Batman No. 1 that had been an exhibit in a copyright case, and it never went back to its original owner. They have court records for other famous cases—including one about The Beatles. They own papers with the original signatures of both Alexander Hamilton and Aaron Burr. There are also court records of the Alger Hiss and Rosenberg trials. They also have court records in the *Titanic* liability case.

Research shelves at the National Archive.

Famous users of their library include Ken Burns and Matthew Broderick, as well as the National Archivist of Finland. They do not have an active digitization program, but they do offer digitization on demand for people who need a JPEG image of a certain resource. I was told that the users of the facility tended to be genealogists, academics, lawyers, and legal historians.

I made my visit before I devised the question of which restaurants the librarians recommend, so I will throw in one of my own. Ulysses' on Pearl Street is a 5- to 10-minute walk and highly recommended.

FURTHER READING

Alexander Hamilton: http://www.titanicinquiry.org/lol/lolh.php.
Batman Issue 1: http://batman.wikia.com/wiki/Batman_Issue_1.
Customs House information: http://www.tripadvisor.com/Attraction_Review-g60763-d116392-Reviews-United_States_Custom_House-New_York_City_New_York.html.
Titanic Inquiry Project: http://www.titanicinquiry.org/lol/lolh.php.

CHAPTER 9

Language Libraries

If it had been possible to build the Tower of Babel without climbing it, it would have been permitted.

Franz Kafka

LIBRARY: JOHN & FRANCINE HASKELL LIBRARY FRENCH INSTITUTE ALLIANCE FRANÇAISE

Address: 22 East 60th Street (between Park and Madison Avenues)
URL: http://www.fiaf.org/library/about.shtml
Telephone: (212) 388-6655
E-mail: library@fiaf.org
Facebook: https://www.facebook.com/fiafny
Twitter: https://twitter.com/fiafny

In the 1970s I worked in the Fine Arts section of the Phoenix Public Library. When times were slow, I would look through the books in ready reference. Once I was looking through a set of *Film World Annual,* and I noticed a picture of a young girl in a Paris park in semiprofile. Later I saw the same picture in the newspaper with the news that the film *The Aviator's Wife* would be shown that night in Scottsdale. My wife and I went, and I thought the film was wonderful. The director, Éric Rohmer, showed a world in France in which young people were all kidding themselves, and your job as the audience was to determine what they were really all about. I became a fan of Rohmer for life and even created a Website for other Rohmer fans. They even quoted me in the *Irish Times* when Rohmer died. I have been to France only once, but it left a lasting impression on me. When I first visited the French Institute Alliance Française library to set up an appointment, I felt like I was entering a slice of Paris on the Upper East Side. There are lots of white and red, comfortable chairs and marble statues of Americans, such as Benjamin Franklin.

50 Specialty Libraries of New York City
ISBN 978-0-08-100554-5

Weeks later, I met with Katharine Branning, Vice President of the Library, who took an hour out to tell me the story of her library. The tale begins in 1911, when The Museum of French Art, the French Institute in the United States was founded, with a provision in its charter for the establishment of a library. Like most of the older institutions I visited, the first incarnation was in Lower Manhattan. True to their word, the library appeared a year later along with the museum. The library served up information on French arts, sciences, and literature for Institute members and the general public. By 1915, the Institute had moved up to 48th Street and Fifth Avenue. By this time it had established a circulating literary library for members only.

Main reading area of the library.

I always ask about famous people who have visited a library, but Branning had information that trumped everyone else. The artist and writer Marcel Duchamp worked at the library when he arrived in New York in 1915, and he stayed there for two years. It is said that he was greatly responsible for the organization of the library.

A decade later the library was moved into a building on East 60th Street, where it remains to this day. By this time, the collection of around 10,000 titles was substantially centered on French decorative arts, but they were starting to build a collection of literature as well. The library weathered the Depression years with decreased hours and a nonexistent budget for new acquisitions. At this point, the nonfiction collection had all been reference, but they loosened this restriction and now all titles could be borrowed by members.

By the early 1950s, the library was in a sad state, and an effort was made to improve working conditions and stop relying on gifts to expand the collection, although a professional librarian was not hired until the 1960s. In 1971 the French Institute merged with the Alliance Française de New York, which had been founded in 1848, and became the French Institute Alliance Française, or FIAF, and the library enjoyed decades of prosperity, becoming the first department of the Institute to get a computer and e-mail. In 1995 the library was further upgraded, thanks to a challenge grant by the French Ministry of Foreign Affairs. This enhancement also included a restructuring of the collection to concentrate on the current image of contemporary France and devote fewer resources to the historical aspect. The final result of this was a complete reconstruction of the library and computerization of the operation. The new library was inaugurated by Catherine Trautmann, Culture Minister of France in 1998. In addition to the library, the FIAF includes a 170-seat amphitheater and a 400-seat full theater.

Currently, the library has 2500 subscribing members, and the library's services are offered to the users of the Institute's many educational programs. During Branning's time at the library, they have developed a major program for juvenile services. A $95 fee entitles members to use all library services, including book circulation, and gives them access to the library's digital collection of e-books and 250 online periodicals. It also grants them free admission to the weekly screenings of French films. The library now owns more than 45,000 titles, with a major collection of books focusing on France in all subject areas. Branning told me that most of the books are in French, although there are also titles in English about France. In addition, they have a substantial collection of language learning materials in all formats. There is also a large collection of French films on DVD.

Branning has been the library director here for 20 years. She has seen the major upgrades and also steered the library through some tough times. She is intense about her advocacy for this library—she gave me the impression that she is awake nights thinking of new ways to move the library forward. I asked her some of the standard questions, such as which item they consider to be their flagship holding, but I was told that they no longer keep rare books, so all the holdings here serve the practical purpose of promoting the French experience, and there is no one title that they are particularly proud of. Famous people who have used the library include the President of France, actress Catherine Deneuve, and authors Gay Talese and Louis Auchincloss.

LIBRARY: GOETHE-INSTITUT

Address: 30 Irving Place, New York, NY 10003
URL: https://www.goethe.de/ins/us/en/sta/ney/bib.html
Telephone: (212) 439-8688
E-mail: circulation@newyork.goethe.org
Access: Browsing open to the public; circulation of books and media for a modest membership fee
Facebook: https://www.facebook.com/goetheinstitut.nyc?fref=ts
Twitter: https://twitter.com/GI_NewYork

Every family has someone who steps up and maintains information about their family tree. This is usually a thankless job (9/10 of my family could not care less). I have done enough of it to know that most of my family is composed of people from the Deep South who did not make much money and were not good at talking to the census man. The one exception is my mother's side, which we have traced back to my great great grandparents, who were German immigrants. I did not know this in college when I took German from the delicate-natured Frau Koppock. I took German because I had a fantasy that I would somehow pass higher math and become an astronomer. I passed the two-year language mark, even though I was not very good at it. The point is that I have a German connection, however slight.

Timing sometimes works in my favor. When I first started contacting the Institute, they were closed for renovation. I sent a note out and heard that they expected to reopen well before my library visit time was complete, so we kept in contact. My visit was eventually set for mid–April, after they had been open in their new location for three weeks.

Library entrance: I thought this was a clever idea.

I was met by their librarian, Katherine Lorimer. I was immediately struck by the strikingly attractive design of the library—all white walls and hardwood shelving, with a bust of Goethe himself by the door.

Goethe among his works.

I am told that the building itself used to be a Rosicrucian Hall and that it was full of mysterious images all over the walls. This is the third location for the library. At first it was housed in a mansion across the street from the Metropolitan Museum. It was a fabulous building, but never quite right for serving as a library. In 2009 the Institute was moved to SoHo, where it was housed on a high floor in an office building. It suffered from a lack of visibility. This was not the case when it was moved to Irving Place; there was a line down the street to get in on opening day. When those people came in, they were immediately presented with a reception desk, which struck me as a great way to humanize a library. It is a fact that libraries can be intimidating, even to other librarians, so touches like this are pure gold.

Periodicals area.

To the left of that door, a double-width display rack of periodicals shows the latest issue of time-tested magazines like *Stern* and *Der Spiegel*. That side of the room also contains a meeting room that comfortably seats about 100 guests for readings and movies. The room is bordered by shelves of books that can be swiveled to allow more or less inclusiveness in the meeting room.

I was told that there are about 8000 physical books and an equal number of e-books. About 80% of these are in German and the rest are English books about Germany. There is no one book that they are particularly proud of, given the nature of the library—they provide good contemporary information on their subject and do not have a rare books effort. They *do* have a wide variety of formats, including a substantial collection of DVDs. Lorimer told me that three-week loans of DVDs are a part of library membership ($10 per person and half-price for seniors like myself). "One problem is that most of these are in PAL format, so you need a special machine to play them," she told me. I lit up at this point because I have such a machine to play my Éric Rohmer films from France. Also, I noted that they had an entire shelf of my favorite German director, Werner Herzog.

Their online catalog is part of the vast German language consortium, and their holdings are included in WorldCat. They use modified Dewey for their nonfiction, which seems to be a minority of the collection. Famous visitors in recent times include Wallace Shawn, famous for *My Dinner with Andre* and *The Princess Bride,* as well as author Günter Grass. Back in the 5th Avenue days they remember celebrities such as Andy Warhol and the German film director Rainer Werner Fassbender.

The Institute does not just passively support German literature. They are involved in an annual contest to find the best translators of German works into English. The Gutekunst Prize is awarded each year to a promising young translator. They also have an active program of language classes, and the library supplies materials in all formats to support the curriculum. To me, this appears to be a blend of library and neighborhood so perfect as to seem magical.

LIBRARY: INSTITUTO CERVANTES

Address: 211 East 49th Street, New York, NY 10017
URL: http://nyork.cervantes.es/en/library_spanish/library_spanish.htm
Telephone: (212) 308-7720, Ext. 4
E-mail: bibny@cervantes.org

Access: Open to the public; circulation for members
Facebook: https://www.facebook.com/InstitutoCervantesNewYork?
fref=ts

I made a preliminary visit to Instituto Cervantes late in winter when I was visiting other libraries on the Upper East Side. Even knowing the street address, I almost walked past the location. You walk down a corridor and end up in a beautiful courtyard, which manages to invoke the feel of a Spanish mansion. Above the library entrance there is a porcelain cat sitting on the roof.

Library seen from the courtyard.

I went in and introduced myself. The man behind the circulation desk alerted the library director, Carmen Delibes, that I was writing a book about specialty libraries and would like to set up a meeting to talk with someone in authority. Five minutes later, I was upstairs. Delibes's desk was at the end of the book stacks with no barrier between her and her patrons. I thought that sent a very appropriate message. She struck me as a young, thoughtful, and soft-spoken person, although at my age most people seem young. She could not answer questions that day, but we did set up a meeting later in the spring.

When I came back to visit her, she was ready with three pages of information addressing my questions. The building dated back to a carpenter's shop in the 1870s, and after many restorations, the site was purchased by the Spanish government in 1999 and totally remodeled to include a library, classrooms, and offices. The library dated back to 1979, but it opened its doors to the public on a 42nd Street location in 1994. In 2003, the library was relocated to its current spot and named after the author Jorge Luis Borges. I was impressed with that choice, as Borges and I share an August birthday. Since then, typical users have included the general public, students, Hispanists, and scholars. It is entirely open to the public during operating hours. Members may check out books and audio for 14 days or movies for 7 days. Basic membership fees are $75 for adults or $35 for seniors and students.

Part of the Borges Library's extensive media collection.

The size of the collection is 75,000 monographs and magazines, 8000 videos, and 5000 audio recordings. The Jorge Luis Borges Library is part of the Instituto Cervantes Library Network, RBIC, the most extensive network of Spanish libraries in the world, and one of the most important open-access Spanish language libraries in the United States. The online catalog at the library displays the holdings for all of the libraries.

1st floor book stacks.

The library wants you to know that they offer unique resources and reference works for students and teachers of Spanish, including specialized dictionaries for studies on literature and the history of the language as well as for research on texts from across Spain and the Americas. In addition there are basic general collections in philosophy, social sciences, art, music, linguistics, geography, and history. The areas of the collection that the library is particularly proud of include Spanish and Latin American literature and the major collection of films and audiovisual materials. After our talk, I was given a tour by Assistant Librarian Richard Heyer. As we were moving through the three floors he gave me one of my better leads for another library to visit—the Hispanic Society in far north Manhattan. That turned into a very valued visit, so this library did its job as an excellent source of information.

LIBRARY: ITALIAN CULTURAL INSTITUTE

Address: 686 Park Avenue, New York, NY 10065
URL: http://www.iicnewyork.esteri.it/IIC_NewYork/Menu/La_
Biblioteca/
Telephone: (212) 879-4242
E-mail: iicnewyork@esteri.it
Access: Open to the public
Facebook: https://www.facebook.com/pages/Italian-Cultural-Institute/
178877595493731?fref=ts
Transportation: Subway line 6 to Hunter College

In several cases I ran up against libraries that were currently closed to the public owing to renovation. For some of these, the libraries were left out of the book because they would not be open for a substantial time. In the case of the Goethe and Italian Institutes, I was able to visit around the time of the reopening.

I learned that the library is part of a network of Italian Cultural Institutes found the world over. The library was established in 1961 by a Columbia professor. It is named after Lorenzo Da Ponte, a lyricist who worked with Mozart on what are, arguably, his three greatest operas— *Don Giovanni, The Marriage of Figaro,* and *Cosí Fan Tutte.* In a very long and somewhat bizarre career, Da Ponte became a priest, took a mistress, fathered two children, was convicted of immorality, and was banished from Venice for 15 years. Eventually, he ended up in the United States, where he taught music at what was then Columbia College. The librarians told me that he was the first Columbia professor to earn tenure.

When I asked what holding they are most proud of, I was told that they own very early editions of the *Divine Comedy,* including one illustrated by Botticelli. The 10,000 books in the reading room are not arranged in Dewey or Library of Congress order, and there are 15,000 more books in nonpublic stacks in the floors above. There used to be more books, but there was a major reorganization in 2000 that caused them to deaccession quite a few titles. Their online catalog is part of the worldwide Italian Cultural Institute network.

Main public collection area.

I asked which famous person had used the library and was told that Jennifer Beals had once been in. Like most librarians, they were eager to talk about which restaurants they recommend to their researchers. "Anything on Lexington Avenue" was the first response, and then they got more specific. "Bernstein's Deli on Third is great." There were also raves for Mariella Pizza.

FURTHER READING

Article about Da Ponte: https://en.wikipedia.org/wiki/Lorenzo_Da_Ponte.
Bernstein's Deli: http://pjbernstein.com/.
Eric Rohmer page: http://www.terryballard.org/rohmer.htm.
George Luis Borges article: http://www.britannica.com/biography/Jorge-Luis-Borges.
Gutekunst Translation Prize: http://www.goethe.de/ins/us/lp/kul/mag/lit/gut/enindex.htm.
The Internet Culturale: http://www.internetculturale.it/opencms/opencms/it/.
Johann Wolfgang von Goethe: http://www.britannica.com/biography/Johann-Wolfgang-von-Goethe.
Making sense of Marcel Duchamp: http://www.understandingduchamp.com/.
Mariella Pizza: http://www.menupages.com/restaurants/mariella-pizza-4/.
Werner Herzog: http://www.wernerherzog.com.
Yelp review of FIAF: http://www.yelp.com/biz/french-institute-alliance-fran%C3%A7aise-new-york-4?osq=fiaf+library.
Yelp review of Instituto Cervantes: http://www.yelp.com/biz/instituto-cervantes-new-york-2.

CHAPTER 10

Services to the Blind

LIBRARY: XAVIER SOCIETY FOR THE BLIND

Address: 2 Penn Plaza, No. 1102, New York, NY 10121
URL: http://www.xaviersocietyfortheblind.org/
Telephone: (212) 473-7800
E-mail: info@xaviersocietyfortheblind.org
Access: Services by mail and Internet download at no charge to qualified visually impaired citizens
Facebook: https://www.facebook.com/pages/Xavier-Society-for-the-Blind/45289787681?fref=ts

It had always been my plan to include a library that provided services for the visually impaired. This is personal for me because I have always been substantially blind in my left eye. If something ever happened to my right eye, I would be facing a very different kind of lifestyle. The best-known service in New York City was Lighthouse International on the Upper East Side. They were hard to reach, but that is not unusual in this project. When I finally did talk to an administrator there, I was told that Lighthouse no longer provided a library for braille and talking books. My estimable colleague at the College of New Rochelle, Sister Martha Counihan, OSU, suggested the Xavier Society. This solved two problems, because I was also looking for a Catholic library (one university in the outer boroughs was known to be relaxed about letting nonstudents into their library for reference, but they did not want to advertise this by being in my book).

I found out that the Xavier Society for the Blind had recently moved from a building in Chelsea to the complex at Penn Station. I liked the location, because I always arrive in the city on the Long Island Railroad, ending at Penn Station. I called the director, Father John Sheehan, SJ, and set up a visit on a Friday in mid-March. Even on the phone, Father John was someone that I was instantly comfortable with, so I knew I was in for a fascinating session.

The Society is on the 11th floor of 2 Penn Plaza, sharing office space with the American Foundation for the Blind (AFB). Father John was waiting by the door when I arrived, in the display area of the Helen Keller Archive, maintained by the AFB. After I put my bags in his office, and coffee was provided, we sat

50 Specialty Libraries of New York City
ISBN 978-0-08-100554-5

down and I encouraged him to tell his story. What a story it was. He has had a varied career, working in the South Pacific and Nigeria. His office is lined with wood carvings and stuffed rhinoceros from his 12 years in Africa. He told me that as a young actor (before entering the Jesuits), he once spent a night of postperformance celebration with Richard Burton. After considerable celebrating, Burton began singing a selection of Welsh songs from his childhood.

Father John Sheehan.

Father John was appointed CEO and director of the Xavier Society in 2008, when the society operated a standard library to check out braille, large-print, and talking books to certified visually impaired patrons. The organization had been founded in 1900 to provide religious and spiritual materials that other agencies were not providing. Xavier was on solid footing financially, but then the economy collapsed, and they found themselves in an unsustainable position. To survive at all, Father John had to reconceptualize the operation, sell the building in Chelsea that they owned, and relocate as a slimmed-down provider of data to blind users. This involved layoffs of more than half of the staff. "It was not the best day of my life," he told me. They were able to soften the blow by providing severance based on the years of service. He was able to cut a deal with the AFB for office space at Penn Plaza. Now the emphasis was on providing braille material to their client base without stipulating that they give it back, providing some audio material for online download, and enlarging the library offerings for audio books.

Father John told me that in the old days, expensive studio equipment was needed to record books and periodicals, but now the technology is good enough that a large web of volunteers can do the recording using their own home computers and send the results in to the organization, from which they are made available through the Society's Web site for direct download. The process is so efficient that many materials could be available to blind users ahead of the actual publication date. As a registered library in the National Library System (Library of Congress), they can also lend audio books to clients.

One of the Society's many awards-printed in Braille and visual fonts.

"Braille is still the primary focus." Father John said that reading works differently on the brain than listening to the same passage in an audio recording, because the recording makes certain choices that cancel the listener's right to imagine. It is not as destructive to the imagination as a filmed version of a book, but the same principle is at work here. In the new system, braille readers are encouraged to keep the books and material the Society provides, rather than returning them as they had in the past. To help encourage young blind children, they have been working to expand the selection of books for children of all ages.

High speed Braille machine.

I was told that there are exciting things in technology to serve the needs of blind readers. For instance, there are renewable braille readers—devices that have pins that pop up to create a line of braille text. When you change the line, the pins fall down and then pop up to create the next.

As far as I could tell, Father John's past experiences did not involve services to the blind, so he went on a mission to walk in their shoes and became a passionate advocate for the visually handicapped. "With the right training and equipment, a blind person can do anything that a fully sighted person can—up to and including driving a car," he said. I was told about blind people bowling and playing golf. To help practice what he preaches, he spent several weeks at the Louisiana Center for the Blind, undergoing training, and he still practices his skill by going for walks wearing his sleep shades and his long white cane. One time he accidentally brushed into someone and the man yelled—"Watch where you're going. Are you blind?"

After a tour of the Xavier offices I was shown the display room for the Helen Keller Archive. On one side of the room you find Keller's original writing desk and her chair.

Helen Keller's desk.

Nearby there is a display case with an Oscar award statuette given for the 1954 documentary *The Unconquered*, produced a decade before *The Miracle Worker*. On a nearby wall, there is a framed picture and note from Mark Twain, who was a huge admirer and supporter of Keller. It is said that when Keller first met Mark Twain she exclaimed "I have touched a king." As with all archives, this is just the tip of the iceberg.

Helen Keller's Oscar. This was the first actual Oscar I had ever seen.

This has been an example of how a library can morph into something very different while still maintaining its total commitment to serving the information needs of its users. It just takes imagination, a thick skin, and a determined leader to make it happen.

LIBRARY: ANDREW HEISKELL BRAILLE AND TALKING BOOK LIBRARY

Address: 40 West 20th Street, New York, NY 10011
URL: http://www.nypl.org/locations/heiskell
Telephone: (212) 206-5400

Access: Open to the public, although special registration required for some services

Facebook: https://www.facebook.com/nyplheiskell?ref=br_rs

Transportation: Subway N&R line, 23rd Street

I visited the Heiskell Library briefly after talking with several people who provide services for the visually handicapped. From what I heard, it seemed that the Heiskell is the best bet for someone who needed braille, a talking book, or large type in a traditional library setting. The library is situated in a pleasant Gramercy neighborhood, surrounded by considerable dining choices. I walked in during a very cold wet morning and was very courteously greeted by the security guard at the door. After walking past the circulation desk and the reference complex I could see what was special about this library.

Notably, the shelves were full of large-type books. As a senior citizen, pushing 70, with one eye that is nearly blind, this is the level of service that would affect me currently. After two cataract surgeries I have learned the fine art of taking care of my one good eye. I could see a section of braille books, but I suspect that these were the current ones and many more are likely in storage.

There is a small but well-stocked section with current magazines. I sat down and read restaurant reviews for a time. While there I noticed that there are lots of rooms off to the side for activities like the recording of talking books. This is a library that seems to have found its niche in the neighborhood and in the larger expanse of the city for people with special needs.

FURTHER READING

Fr. John at the Louisiana Center for the Blind: http://xaviersocietyfortheblind.blogspot.com.

IPad Braille keyboard: http://www.wired.com/2015/01/ibrailler-ipad-app/.

News story about the changing status of the organization: http://www.catholicnews.com/data/stories/cns/1202841.htm.

Refreshable Braille display: http://en.wikipedia.org/wiki/Refreshable_braille_display.

The Unconquered, a documentary about Helen Keller: http://www.imdb.com/title/tt0048157/?ref_=nm_flmg_slf_2.

CHAPTER 11

Science

The good thing about science is that it's true whether or not you believe in it.

Neil deGrasse Tyson

LIBRARY: AMERICAN MUSEUM OF NATURAL HISTORY RESEARCH LIBRARY

Address: Central Park West at 79th Street
URL: http://www.amnh.org/our-research/research-library
Telephone: (212) 769-5100
E-mail: libref@amnh.org
Access: Open to the general public from 2:00 to 5:30 Tuesday, Wednesday, and Thursday
Facebook: https://www.facebook.com/sharer/sharer.php?u=http%3A%2F%2Fwww.amnh.org%2Four-research%2Fresearch-library%2Fabout-the-library
Flickr: https://www.flickr.com/search/?q=american%20museum%20of%20natural%20history
YouTube: https://www.youtube.com/user/AMNHorg
Transportation: Subway: B & C lines, 81st Street. Bus: M79

I visited the American Museum of Natural History (AMNH) library in April 2015. I am a museum member, so that made it extra easy when I had to show the guards my ID before I went up to the top floor to see the library. With its whales, dinosaurs, dioramas, planetarium, gift shop, and IMAX theater, the museum is a wildly popular stop in New York City. The tone of the crowd is more like Macy's the week before Christmas than a somber institution of learning.

I have tried in vain to visit the museum at an off hour, but on this day the library was practically empty—it was a Friday, so museum goers cannot just walk in like they can from Tuesday through Thursday. I was there to meet Tom Baione, whose official title is Harold Boeschenstein Director, Department of Library Services, AMNH. Also, the reference librarian, Mai

50 Specialty Libraries of New York City
ISBN 978-0-08-100554-5

Reitmeyer, who had first discussed my visit, was there that day. Even though the library was mostly empty, it was still humming with intense reference questions over the phone, so I had several minutes to look around the shelves and check out exhibits like the glass case with a detailed model of the HMS *Beagle*. The reference books were all cataloged using Library of Congress classification, supported by an Innovative Interfaces, Inc., online catalog (III catalogs are the mark of a library that is truly prospering). On the east wall near the reference desk, there is a large metal plate with an original page of *Birds of America*.

Copper plate of Birds in America.

The reading room is spacious, well lit, and appealing. It is the tip of a giant information iceberg.

Main public reading area.

When Baione was finally finished with telephone reference, he took me on an energetic and eye-opening trip through Wonderland. The library began in 1869 with the founding of the museum by Theodore Roosevelt's father and others. An annex building was constructed in 1993 to house an enormous collection of books, journals, portable dioramas, photographs, model dinosaurs, motion pictures, manuscripts, and memorabilia.

Past the card catalog (still accurate, though not updated since 1993) the first stop is the new acquisitions room, where new titles are available for inspection by the museum's faculty members, who number in the hundreds. A second room contains recent acquisitions of paper periodicals. Baione said that the library is moving heavily in the direction of electronic journals for its thousands of subscriptions, and most of the paper titles that are left are either journals that do not publish online or, more likely, journals that sell only subscriptions that include both formats.

Further in, there was a room for preview of new paper journals, and clearly there were a lot of empty shelves. "We are going to reassign some of this space to reflect the new realities of library service," I was told. We walked through an area with seemingly dozens of scanning stations feeding a massive digitization program. Then we were off to the elevators to visit a dizzying array of staff-only floors filled with compact shelving—and treasures beyond description.

The first stop was a room with giant floor-to-ceiling freezer cabinets. These were for the preservation of nitrate negatives, which famously disintegrate in upsetting ways if they are not properly maintained. Baione said that the negatives need to be relocated every other year so that the freezers can be defrosted.

Next we saw a room with racks of motion picture films, many or most of them in 16-mm format. There was also storage for glass-plate negatives. The standard size was 8 by 10 inches, although a few special landscape camera negatives were as big as the windows in my house. Further along there was a large collection of videos. If you were an audiovisual education student in the 1980s you know what is meant by 3/4 inch Umatic format, and the rest of you have not missed much. Obviously, the library is interested in saving these to a more friendly format, but with this much to do, priorities must be established. More shelves contained lantern slides with scripts. These were the forebears of the film strips that we used in the 1950s, which begat slide/tape sets and finally video. This floor also contained a large selection of portable dioramas about the size of a medium suitcase that circulated to schools in the area.

Dioramas to go.

The memorabilia area is figuratively, if not literally, filled with the ghost of Charles R. Knight. Baione described him as the Dinosaur Whisperer. Knight could look at a fossil skeleton and see what any of the old creatures looked like, and he had the artistic talent to bring this to life for the rest of us. Most of the models fit on a standard library shelf, ranging from tiny up to the size of a standard poodle. Many of them look eerily real. Another floor contained many ranges to hold the papers of Neil deGrasse Tyson, the museum's media superstar. This was a logical choice for his archive because Tyson grew up in Brooklyn and got his first look at the stars inside the Hayden Planetarium. Afterward, they say, he grew up with the museum.

By this time, after covering eight floors of holdings, I had no sense of direction or height, but eventually we were in the storage room next to the reference desk. The room contains cabinets full of photographic prints. I was told that there were more than a million, and that 10,000 of them had been digitized so far.

Photography files.

As a librarian with a history of digitization work, I approve of this ratio. It is good practice to digitize enough to get people interested and motivate them to visit the library and hold the originals in their hands. At the end of the room, as you walk back to the reference desk, you see a sight that helped me summarize the experience of visiting this library. In front of me was a large model of a dinosaur, probably a brontosaurus. Behind that, on the next range of shelves rested a rather weather-beaten sled. "That's something that Peary brought back from the Arctic," Baione told me.

Items from the past and the far past.

The collection of nearly half a million books is reference-only to museum visitors, but AMNH faculty members may borrow them, even titles in the rare books collection. They take the title "faculty" very literally, since the museum has a long-standing partnership with Columbia University. Also, the most surprising fact of my visit concerns the museum's educational program. They have two degree-granting programs. One is a Ph.D. in comparative biology. The second is a Master's degree program to send science teachers out to the local community. Students must have a bachelor's degree in earth science, and they must not have any teaching experience. The few lucky students who enroll here are taught entirely by in-house faculty members, and they are farmed out to schools in the area who are highly motivated to hire them. Also, there is no tuition for this program.

The library regularly works with the museum staff to create displays based on their holdings. Some of this work inspired a series of beautiful full-color books, displayed at the reference desk. Tom went to the back to bring out a copy of *Natural Histories*, and autographed it to me. Not for the first time in this project I left feeling very proud to be a librarian and very proud to be a New Yorker.

LIBRARY: THE EXPLORERS CLUB

Address: 46 East 70th Street, New York, NY 10021
URL: https://explorers.org/about/research/library
Telephone: (212) 628-8383
E-mail: researchcollections@explorers.org
Access: By advance appointment
Facebook: https://www.facebook.com/pages/The-Explorers-Club/691604090855340
Twitter: https://twitter.com/explorersclub

Since my early teen years I have been an amateur astronomer and armchair explorer. I followed the space program every day as we went from 15-minute flights over the atmosphere to that day in August of 1969 when Neil Armstrong and Buzz Aldrin walked on the moon. My favorite movie in those days was *Lawrence of Arabia*. On a similar note, favorite books included titles like Geoffrey Moorhouse's *The Fearful Void*, about a camel trek across the Sahara. Despite the obvious connection to my interests, the Explorers Club was not on my first list because access looked a bit too restrictive. As in the case of most libraries, they turned out to be very welcoming.

The entrance to the Club was so unassuming that I walked right past it, but double-checked the address before I crossed the wrong street. The first sight is of an elegant mansion, completely wood paneled. In the room to the left there are display cases with items from an arctic expedition and models of NASA vehicles. Straight ahead on the way to the elevator, there is a very large world globe that I would find out later was used by Thor Heyerdahl to plot his trip across the Pacific. The elevator was one of those antiques that was, I suspected, original equipment.

On the fifth floor I knocked at the door to the library and archive and was quickly met by Lacey Flint, a young and enthusiastic archivist. I soon found out that the library owns 14,000 volumes, 1400 of which are considered to be rare. The organization has been around for more than a century, and there was a library from the beginning—it was a small library of about 50 volumes until the 1920s, when most of the volumes came into the collection via James B. Ford, member and past Club president. The charter members of the organization included David Legge Brainard, survivor of the Lady Franklin Bay Expedition of 1881, and Frederick Cook, surgeon to the Peary expedition to the Arctic.

When I first sat down, I noticed a block of wood about six inches wide and high, with a brass marker on the front. I asked about that, and was told that it was a piece of balsa from the original Kon Tiki.

Kon Tiki remnant.

When I asked my standard question about which famous person had used the library, I was told that their visitors included most of the men who had been to the moon. Stephen Hawking had met with club officials and "signed" a copy of his book by adding an inked thumbprint.

Hawkings' "autograph" of his book.

Eventually we walked up half a flight of stairs to the Trophy Room, which reminded me quite a bit of the trophy room at Theodore Roosevelt's Sagamore Hill. Flint said that the room should remind me of Roosevelt because the long table in the center of the room was used by the president to plan the construction of the Panama Canal.

The Trophy Room.

She then set up a foam book holder to show off the library's most prized possession—a multivolume set of reports from Napoleon's 1799 expedition to Egypt. In addition to troops, he brought along a large force of scientists, archaeologists, and artists to record what they could find of the antiquities. The volumes, published substantially in full color, are magnificent.

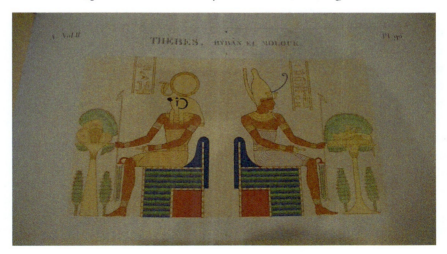

A portion of Napoleon's Egypt report.

Flint asked me "Do you hear that grinding sound?" I did, and it seemed to be coming from the fireplace. "When I first started working here, we were in the room at night and I was starting to wonder." We were getting into an area that I wanted to cover at many libraries but never had the nerve to ask. "Any ghostly activities in your 100-year-old library?" In this case, the answer turned out to be more prosaic. The sound of the weather vane atop the roof was drifting down the fireplace.

Guardian of the Trophy Room.

We went back to the archive and finished talking. I asked about a box on the shelves nearby labeled "Roosevelt." These turned out to be lantern slides of Theodore Roosevelt's various journeys. They were hand-tinted views of his trip to the Nile, as well as images of his postpresidential visit to the Amazon region, where he led a team of American and Brazilian explorers down an Amazon tributary known as the River of Doubt, because nobody at the time knew exactly where it went. There is a shot of him staring proudly at the camera as the expedition was about to begin. It turned out to be the most dangerous and grueling expedition of his life, and not everybody made it back. Owing to exhaustion, starvation, and illness, Roosevelt was almost one of the casualties.

Roosevelt lantern slides.

After my visit, I went downstairs past the world globe that had been used by Thor Heyerdahl and took Flint up on her offer of coffee. Sitting in the reception room, I was surrounded by models of NASA spacecraft and relics from Polar expeditions. As the receptionist made me a fresh pot of coffee, I could not help but think, "This is as good as it gets."

FURTHER READING

Charles R. Knight, dinosaur artist: http://www.charlesrknight.com/AMNH.htm.
Charles R. Knight's Prehistoric Vision: http://www.smithsonianmag.com/science-nature/charles-r-knights-prehistoric-visions-16099537/?no-ist/.
Eleven awesome things you can see at the Explorers Club: http://mentalfloss.com/article/57025/11-awesome-things-you-can-see-explorers-club.
Neil DeGrasse Tyson official page: http://www.haydenplanetarium.org/tyson/.
Tom Baione's book "Natural Histories." https://www.waterstones.com/book/natural-histories/tom-baione/9781454912149.
YouTube Video "Inside the Explorers Club:" https://www.youtube.com/watch?v=z6YrFs1DKNA.

CHAPTER 12

Entertainment

R.K. Maroon: How much do you know about show business, Mr. Valiant?
Eddie Valiant: Only that there is no business like it, no business I know.
From Who Framed Roger Rabbit?

LIBRARY: THE HAMPDEN-BOOTH THEATRE LIBRARY, THE PLAYERS FOUNDATION FOR THEATRE EDUCATION

Address: 16 Gramercy Park South, New York, NY 10003
URL: http://www.hampdenbooth.org/
Telephone: (212) 228-1861
E-mail: http://www.hampdenbooth.org/contact.php
Access: Open to qualified researchers by appointment
Transportation: Subway lines 4 and 6 to 23rd Street

The Players Club had not been on the original list I compiled of libraries to visit. We had seen the building a few times and looked at it with reverence—it was one of the most historic sites in the city. Founded by Edwin Booth, it had Mark Twain and William Tecumseh Sherman as founding members. When visiting the Masonic Library, I had been tipped off that The Players Club had a library that had some access to the public. I checked and found to my happy surprise that this was correct. I quickly e-mailed the librarian, Raymond Wemmlinger, and set up an appointment for April 1—the only day I would attempt to visit four libraries.

Portrait gallery in the living room.

I was met by Wemmlinger, who looked every inch the part for the role he had been playing for four decades. He is tall with white hair and a Shakespearean voice. He led me into the living room with stained-glass windows looking toward the Square. "This is the original building that Edwin Booth procured in 1888, but this part of it was redesigned by Stanford White, creating a porch and vestibule." Even without that connection, the room is sheer magic. There are portraits of Kate Hepburn, José Ferrer, and Peter O'Toole. "Ferrer was a past president and frequent user of the library," Wemmlinger said. Other famous visitors included the author John Jakes and the actress Helen Hayes, who had been the first woman admitted to the Club in 1988.

Portrait of Edwin Booth.

Edwin Booth had felt that theater people did not get the respect they deserved as serious artists, so he collected every book he could find to dispel that idea, and that became the heart of the library, which was founded as part of the original Club. Booth also contributed his letters (more than 2000 written by Booth or to him), scrapbooks, and "prompt books." Also, he felt that actors tended to hang out with other actors, so he saw the Club as a way for actors to socialize with other distinguished citizens, such as writers and politicians, and thus be accepted in that kind of league.

You might think that an organization formed by and for society's greatest celebrities would not have to worry about money, but you would be surprised. In 2014, the Club put a John Singer Sargent portrait of Jefferson up for sale to raise $2 million, even though the painting had been part of an early bequest from Booth. In 2000, the Club's finances were in such a state that it came to the attention of the state Attorney General. Although there was a lengthy inquiry, there were no crimes uncovered, although it did lead to a restructuring of the organization, with the Club coexisting with the educational foundation that included the library.

Shakespearean stained glass in the dining hall.

Up the stairs, and we went past too many portraits to describe, although the one at the reading room door stood out—Mark Twain. The reading room is a rectangular gem of an ornate, wood-paneled library room. It is a frequent meeting place for public programs. A table at the west end of the room contained postcard-sized pictures of actresses. "We have photos of every actress who ever walked on a Broadway stage—12,000 in all," said Wemmlinger. A frequent favorite of researchers is the set of two photographs of Evelyn Nesbit, the beauty whose charms led to the death of Stanford White by a jealous husband.

Library Reading Room.

Farther up the stairs, past portraits of Emmett Kelly and Norman Rockwell, there is a floor that was, until the 1980s, devoted to housing actors who were in town temporarily. Those floors were taken over by the library and archive. These higher floors contain the rare books, such as the original Booth Collection and his letters and scrapbooks. This contains playbills and notices about Booth's performances over a half-century, ending in a farewell performance of Hamlet in 1891 at the Brooklyn Academy.

The top floor was an apartment where Booth spent the last few years of his life. On his bedroom wall there are portraits of all of his relatives, including the one whose name he would not speak after 1865. The room also contains three human skulls, used in various productions of Hamlet. Holding up one of them, Wemmlinger asked "Do you know who this is?" I was an English major in my day, so I said "Certainly—it's Yorick, a man of infinite jest." One of those skulls is that of a criminal who saw Booth in Hamlet, just before the law caught up with him. His last request before being hanged was to donate his skull to Booth, who gratefully accepted.

One of three skulls used by Booth in performances of Hamlet.

Looking out over Gramercy Park, Wemmlinger told the story of the night Booth died. There was a fierce thunderstorm that did not keep throngs of New Yorkers away from the street in front of the house. Just before the end, the power went off, and Booth's daughter exclaimed "Don't let my father die in the dark!" Moments later the lights came back just as Booth slipped into the ages.

I always ask the librarians where they send researchers to lunch when they are spending serious time at the library. Ray recommended Pete's Tavern, which had been in operation for decades when The Players Club was formed.

Mark Twain billiard memorial.

At this point we were all too aware of my next appointment, so Raymond showed me one more thing—down the stairs to street level, and one more to the pool room. Right above the pool table, there is a cue mounted as a trophy. It was Mark Twain's designated cue. It was the perfect end to a visit that was off the charts in the matter of the "wow factor."

LIBRARY: LOUIS ARMSTRONG ARCHIVE

Address: Benjamin S. Rosenthal Library, 65-30 Kissena Boulevard, Queens, NY
URL: http://library.qc.cuny.edu/collections/offsite.php#armstrong
Telephone: (718) 997-3700
E-mail: http://www.louisarmstronghouse.org/about/contact.htm
Access: By appointment
Facebook: https://www.facebook.com/louisarmstronghousemuseum?rf=115407638474907

I had been having trouble finding libraries to cover in Queens, so I was very happy to hear about the special collections at Queens College's Rosenthal Library. In particular, I was happy to visit the Louis Armstrong archives. My son used to have an apartment in Queens a few blocks away from Flushing Cemetery, where Satchmo is laid to rest. His grave is easy to spot—the only one with a marble trumpet resting on the stone. Also, he thoughtfully arranged for a stone bench, so you could linger for a while and have your Louis Armstrong moment.

I had arranged with archivist Ricky Riccardi to drop by on a Wednesday morning in April. The library is in the part of campus farthest from Kissena Boulevard, and when I arrived I announced myself to the security guard, who did not know there was an Armstrong collection. It turned out that the archive is in a room just off to the right of the library entrance. Ricky has been with the collection since 2006 and has been the official archivist since 2009.

Armstrong was an iconic figure in the entertainment world, and he could have lived anywhere he wanted but, in 1943, he chose to buy a house in a working-class neighborhood in Corona, Queens, and lived there until his death in 1971. His wife lived there until 1983 and then donated the house and all of its belongings to the city.

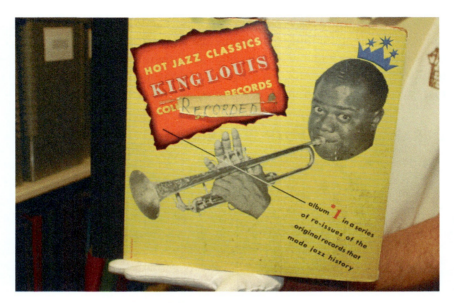

A part of Armstrong's record collection.

After considerable discussion and jockeying about, Queens College stepped up to the plate and opened the archive in 1994. The actual house was opened as a museum a decade later. Riccardi told me that there would be an education center built next to the Armstrong House in a couple of years, and the archive would relocate at that time.

When I asked my standard question about which famous people have visited the site, I was told that Quincy Jones had visited and that Wynton Marsalis had brought his own mouthpiece so he could play one of Satchmo's trumpets.

Armstrong's original trumpets.

Much of the funding comes from the Louis Armstrong Foundation which, itself, still gets a considerable income from royalties. When asked what they considered to be their flagship holding, I was told without hesitation that it was a padded case containing five of Armstrong's original trumpets. A close second is a collection of more than 700 reel-to-reel tapes, containing the sounds of concerts, practice sessions, a few off-color jokes, and even arguments with his wife.

Example of Armstrong's tape collection.

At all times, Armstrong had a keen sense of how important his legacy would be. A number of times on the tapes he could be heard saying "This is for posterity." Naturally, these tapes have already been digitized, and they will be preserved for all time. The only catch is that the estate has not approved the release of these sounds, so I may not hear them in my lifetime.

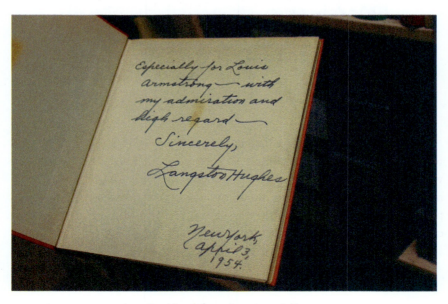

Inscribed book from Armstrong's library.

The archive room also contains shelves full of the books that were in his home library at the time of his death. There were popular novels by Uris and Steinbeck, but also books in which Armstrong was mentioned. Riccardi held out a copy of a Langston Hughes book about black entertainers, and the title page contains a neatly inscribed note to Armstrong by the author, professing his admiration for Armstrong's work. Pretty high praise for a man who had never gone beyond the fifth grade in school; but then Mark Twain held the same educational credentials.

Further along the archives, we see that they have kept every conceivable bit of memorabilia about the man—dolls, buttons, negatives, contact sheets, and concert posters, among many other objects. "We make the claim that has never been disputed that this is the single largest collection about a single jazz musician in the entire world," Riccardi said. The international aspect was emphasized when the archive was awarded a massive collection from a Swedish collector that filled in major gaps in materials about Armstrong's work overseas.

Letter that was actually delivered to Armstrong in Queens.

Eventually we made our way back to the main reading room, and Riccardi brought out a pair of ornate satchels on a library book cart. He opened up the first, which contained a selection of Armstrong's mouthpieces. "The last person to blow through this was Louis Armstrong," he said. No matter how renowned the guest, these were sacred objects. Finally, we reached the payoff. He opened a velvet-bound case with four of the master's trumpets, including the main trumpet with his name etched on the side. I put on white gloves and had the honor of holding the trumpet in my hand.

Holding history in my hands.

Before I left, I asked Riccardi where he would send researchers to lunch if they were making a day of it. "We have food on campus of course, but, well, you know …." I have worked at colleges for 25 years. I know. "We always send people across Kissena Boulevard to Gino's Pizza and Pasta." At least they will for the next two years. A major education center is being built across the street from the Armstrong House in Corona, and that will be the permanent home for those trumpets.

LIBRARY: NEW YORK PUBLIC LIBRARY FOR THE PERFORMING ARTS

Address: 40 Lincoln Center Plaza, New York, NY 10023
URL: http://www.nypl.org/locations/lpa
Telephone: (917) 275-6975
Access: Open to the public
Facebook: https://www.facebook.com/nypl.lpa
Twitter: https://twitter.com/nypl_lpa

This was my first visit to one of the New York Public Library (NYPL) branches that I had targeted for the book, so I blithely walked in one day, announced myself, and asked if I could set up an appointment with someone in authority. Phone calls were made, hushed whispers were whispered, and I was finally given the name of someone, along with a phone number. "She's not here today but call her and she'll be happy to help." I did that, as well as e-mailing her, and finally got one e-mail back letting me know that she was very busy. I am sure she was very busy, because she was the gatekeeper of all contacts with writers for the entire NYPL system. The punch line is that she never did get back to me, so I resorted to plan B. I would take advantage of the fact that I am a card-carrying member of the library system, visit the libraries I needed because they are open to the public, and write what I find. It was sort of like writing a Yelp review.

There was one item at their library that I was very eager to see. It was the original typed script of the movie *East of Eden*, starring James Dean, Julie Harris, and Raymond Massey, directed by Elia Kazan. It was my favorite movie of all time. I had visited the Kazan archives at Wesleyan University in Connecticut, and I had a quick look at the script—enough to know that there are things that were left out of the movie at the last minute. I even have a Web page about the film, so seeing this would give me ammunition for that work. I was directed to visit the second floor and see the reference librarian. He turned out to be a very, very low key information specialist, who stared at his screen for several minutes to verify what I already knew. They had two scripts for *East of Eden*. One was a published version, which was in remote storage. The typed script was, indeed, on their third floor, waiting for me. In the middle of this transaction, Mr. Low Key had to leave for lunch, and he was replaced by a somewhat grim woman. I tried to lighten up the mood by mentioning that I had heard that the Performing Arts Library had videotapes of every Broadway play in the last half-century.

"We don't have *every* play."

"This might be my one chance to see the Steve Martin and Robin Williams' *Waiting for Godot*," I offered.

"Not just anybody can see those videos. You have to have special qualifications." Clearly she did not think I had special qualifications. My listing in Google Scholar shows 70 articles and two books, but I did not want to ruin her day by sharing that information.

I headed off to the third floor to see my script, and she called me back. "You know, don't you, that you can't check this out. You must use it in the library." Gosh, I just landed on your planet and never dreamed of such a thing, I did not say.

On the third floor I had to check my bag, leaving nothing to deal with information but my smartphone and what is left of my brain. I had to fill out a form to request the item, and then another form that explained in some detail who I am and what I was doing here. Despite all of those rules, the people at the special collections desk could not have been nicer. I was supposed to watch the monitor for my number to come up, but the librarian told me to relax and signaled when the item arrived. It was exactly what I had hoped it was, and as I gave it back I mentioned that I would be back at a later time to get a more detailed look. "We will save your information so you won't have to fill everything out again next time," she told me.

On my way out the door, I paused to admire a display of Al Hirschfeld art, including his writing desk. By this time, I had seen the writing desks of four iconic figures. New York is, truly, a city of treasures.

LIBRARY: PALEY CENTER FOR MEDIA

URL: paleycenter.org
Address: 25 West 52nd Street, New York, NY 10019
Telephone: (212) 621-6600
E-mail: ScholarsRoom@paleycenter.org
Access: Open to the public with advance reservation
Facebook: https://www.facebook.com/PaleyCenter
Twitter: https://twitter.com/paleycenter
Transportation: Subway line E to 53rd Street and 5th Avenue

We had visited the Museum of Television and Radio when it opened in its new facility on 53rd Street in 1991. It was a wildly popular tourist site owing to its show business glamor and the fact that you could see television shows from your distant past—just look in their vast catalog and call up whatever you want to see. The museum had existed since the 1970s, but 1991 was when it really came into its own. It was so popular that you had to make your selection and then wait an hour or two for a slot at your viewing station. The museum was a treat in every way, with exhibits and screenings, but it had one overwhelming selling point—this was the only way you could get this information.

Over the years the environment changed somewhat. The Internet appeared in ordinary homes and then the World Wide Web. Something called YouTube came along, which began showing clips of old movies and television shows that users kept on their home computers. I will admit that I had not been to the museum for some time, but I was curious how they coped with this dramatic change of environment. I was delighted to see that they had a Scholars' Room, and further that its manager Mark Ekman was very happy to talk with me about the book. We set up a visit for a Sunday in late Spring. Sunday seemed like an odd choice, but it was great for me because it was easier to get around Midtown on a weekend.

The building is a wonder in itself—designed by Philip Johnson to look like a giant five-story 1940s-style radio. I walked in and was immediately bathed in the glow of media as a wall at the end of the room was showing video feeds from around the world. Mark came down and introduced himself, moving me down the hall to see the enormous lush theater with seating for 200. One oddity he pointed out about the theater is that there is no backstage—all setup work has to be done in advance of a performance.

Next we went to the basement to see the control room, and it looks like a control room that you might see in the film *Network* or the television show *Newsroom*, with giant banks of dials and monitors. It was also where they kept the tapes of their second-tier video archive. The things most likely to be requested are already digitized and in their computer servers, but things that get looked at occasionally are kept on tape and spooled to order on fairly short notice. Tapes that are further down the food chain are kept in a vault through the archival storage company "Iron Mountain." Not "Cold Mountain"—a mistake that I made in the course of the day.

On a higher floor there are several more smaller theaters. They get a lot of visitors from around the world, including an annual VIP tour from China. Often the group leaders look through the selection and pick out videos for their class. Almost as often, once the people arrive and find out what the choices are, the showing can take an entirely new direction. There are many visitors from Europe and a growing number from South America. Sometimes highly specialized groups arrive, such as the George Reeves Fan Club, in honor of television's original Superman. We went back up the elevator and then up to the top of the 11-story building adjacent to the museum. There we saw the Grant Tinker Boardroom, adorned with original artwork by Al Hirschfeld. One group shot of CBS personalities had Alan Funt obviously pasted in. It turned out that he hated the original drawing so much that he threatened dire consequences, so Hirschfeld made him a caricature more to his liking.

Beyond that, we entered the William Paley office. He had one of the more unusual executive desks I have seen—a poker table. At the bottom, there is a pair of women's shoes. "Those are Mrs Paley's," said Ekman. She had said there was nothing feminine there, and she decided to fix that. On the shelves was the kind of giant broadcast microphone that you see in front of Larry King.

Last, we went to the Scholars' Room, which contained banks of wide monitors, which replaced the giant viewing booths of times past. Also, they have, since 2007, rebranded themselves as the Paley Center for Media and expanded their lineup of programming, using their immense contacts with media personalities. On that subject, my usual question about famous people using a library was almost meaningless here. Mark told me that there are so many such occasions that they have well-defined rules for dealing with it. The toughest for him was the period in which Valerie Harper was a regular visitor. She was studying Tallulah Bankhead for an upcoming play. The problem is that he himself was a big fan, who often played episodes of the Mary Tyler Moore show at his desk when working late nights. After weeks of restraint, he finally had the talk with her.

I asked him if they could make some arrangement to allow museum visitors to view some of their treasures off-site, given that all of this was becoming digital. He said that would be a dream come true for them, but the contracts from the copyright owners forbid such a thing, so it remains stuck on the shelf of wish list items.

The Paley Center proves that libraries and archives have the staying power to adapt to the most trying conditions.

LIBRARY: CONJURING ARTS

Address: 11 West 30th Street (just west of 5th Avenue)
URL: http://conjuringarts.org/library/
Telephone: (212) 594-1033
E-mail: librarian@conjuringarts.org
Access: Open to researchers by advance appointment
Facebook: https://www.facebook.com/conjuringartsresearchcenter
Twitter: https://twitter.com/search?q=conjuring%20arts&src=typd

Like many a person before me, I have seen a few magic acts that amazed me, a few that did not, and nothing to make me think that actual magic could be produced on demand for a paying audience. I had set up my appointment with this library thinking that it would be just one more library with a distinct specialty, but it turned out to be one of the most surprising visits of the project.

The library is located on an upper floor in a high-rise building just off of 5th Avenue. It is narrow, so you have to pay attention to the number. The library will give you very detailed instructions on how to buzz them, and I managed to get it after a few tries. I rode up an elevator that was packed with residents and a small but friendly dog. I was met at the floor by the reference librarian and introduced to the library's owner, Bill Kalush, whose business card immediately tips you off that this is no ordinary library founder—the extra-large card contains an image of the King of Spades, as well as the usual type of information.

Part of the library's amazing rare books collection.

The tour starts with a look at the rare books room. This is where things got surprising. Kalush makes it his business to collect any book concerning magical acts, including mind games that were found in the back of mathematical texts. This led to him amassing a collection of incunabula the likes of which I had never seen. He told me that he first caught the bug for this type of research while using the New York Public Library's magic collection, then decided to create his own resource, and

15,000 books later, he has created one of the most significant conjuring collections in the world. This collection is noncirculating, but he also runs several circulating collections out of local magic shops—one for books and another for props.

One of the library's rarest items.

Kalush then added another surprise; going into his technical services area, I saw state-of-the-art equipment and learned that they are running a massive digitization program for their original material from magicians. In one case, they had publications from a magician who used a Ditto machine (readers who grew up in the 1950s will know what I mean), and they had a volunteer rekey the words because they were not of sufficient quality to digitize.

He said that the library was initially self-funded and still takes no government money. More recently, though, they have received private grants for their considerable program in education.

I asked about which famous people have used the library and had no trouble in getting several good answers. The late astronaut Scott Carpenter was a friend of Kalush's and had visited the library. Also, the magician David Copperfield had been by.

FURTHER READING

Al Hirschfeld foundation page: http://www.alhirschfeldfoundation.org/.

Amazon page for Raymond Wemmlinger - http://www.amazon.com/Raymond-Wemmlinger/e/B001JOYCKA/ref=dp_byline_cont_book_1.

East of Eden: A Resource Guide to the Film: http://www.terryballard.org/eastofeden.html.

Encyclopedia Britannica article on Edwin Booth - http://www.britannica.com/EBchecked/topic/73702/Edwin-Booth.

Internet Movie Database biography of Walter Hampden - http://www.imdb.com/name/nm0358899/.

Internet Movie Database listing for Louis Armstrong: http://www.imdb.com/name/nm0001918/.

Louis Armstrong – biography and song selection: http://www.redhotjazz.com/louie.html.

New York Public Library description of Sarum Ellison papers: http://archives.nypl.org/mss/6267.

Philip Johnson: http://www.pritzkerprize.com/biography-philip-johnson.

Wall Street Journal article about the Conjuring library: http://www.wsj.com/articles/SB10001424127887323826704578356542833994224.

William Paley: http://www.britannica.com/biography/William-S-Paley.

CHAPTER 13

Culture

You don't have to burn books to destroy a culture. Just get people to stop reading them.

Ray Bradbury

LIBRARY: CENTER FOR JEWISH HISTORY

Address: 15 West 16th Street
URL: http://www.cjh.org/
Telephone: (212) 294-8301
E-mail: inquiries@cjh.org
Access: Open to the general public
Facebook: https://www.facebook.com/pages/Center-for-Jewish-History/104082532962550?fref=ts
Twitter: @cjewishhistory
Blog: Blog.cjh.org

I visited the Center on April 1—following my visit to The Players Club and preceding my visit to the Center for Fiction and the American Society for Psychical Research. I was met by Laura Leone, Director of Library and Archive Services; David Rosenberg, Reference Services Research Coordinator; and Sacha Evans, PR Consultant. As we walked into the immense lobby, I was shown the Wall of Messages created in 1999.

50 Specialty Libraries of New York City
ISBN 978-0-08-100554-5

Wall of Messages in the Center's library.

Leone explained that the Center is the product of a partnership between five agencies—the American Sephardi Federation, American Jewish Historical Society, Leo Baeck Institute, Yeshiva University Museum, and YIVO Institute for Jewish Research. All of the holdings are described in an online catalog driven by the Ex Libris software named "Aleph." This is overlaid with a discovery layer powered by the Ex Libris Primo software for more intuitive Web access. They told me that their catalog has the capability of adding images to bibliographic records. I checked this out later, using the search "sculpture," and found that the discovery catalog led me to a number of items with the format Visual Material. When you choose one, you get a thorough description of the item, and it provides a further link to the image itself.

With so much to choose from it was hard to answer my standard question about which item is the most prized, but they did mention a letter from Thomas Jefferson explaining his views about religious freedom. The rare book room has 3600 volumes, including a considerable number of incunabula, and access to the room is strictly for high-level staff (normally only six people have access), so I was immensely complimented to be given an inside look at the room.

Major displays are set up along the perimeter of the room. I was told that they are particularly fond of exhibitions that can promote the collections of all of the partner institutions. They said that they would soon be showing a major civil rights exhibit.

Past the rare books, there is a giant computer bank to display some of the treasures that have been digitized by the Center. It runs an automatic slide show, but if something catches your eye, you can pause it and zoom in for a better view.

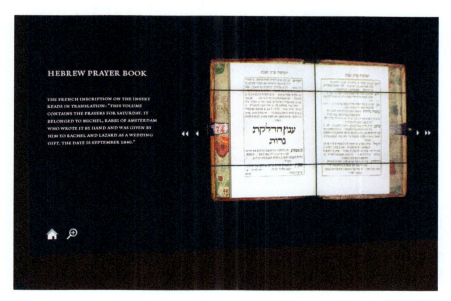

Computer displays of the Center's treasures.

Next we went downstairs to see the nerve center for archival processing, preservation, and digitization. As we arrive at the lower level we see a selection of the Center's large collection of materials about Yiddish theater. They are not necessarily trying to digitize everything they own, but at least they want to create rich finding aids for their content. The digitization area is, quite simply, state of the art. One staff member was digitizing a very fragile, centuries-old book. I was told that they use ABBYY software for optical character recognition of digitized works. I was also impressed that they own microform readers that have OCR software built in. Another staff person was working on digital preservation of oral histories. The Center works very hard to get grants for digitization. When full digital access is not possible, they create finding aids to help people locate the materials when they come into the Lillian Goldman Reading Room.

Book digitization equipment.

Finally, we looked through a glass window at the Werner J. and Gisella Levi Cahnman Preservation Laboratory, where technicians in lab coats were breathing new life into paper documents that had been all but destroyed. The librarians emphasized that all services in the Collection Management Wing are performed for all of the partners.

Materials getting a new life at the Cahnman Preservation Laboratory.

We then went upstairs to see the Lillian Goldman Reading Room and the Ackman & Ziff Family Genealogy Institute. The genealogy room is filled with banks of computers and staffed with experts who can work with anyone from a day one beginner to a seasoned family tree searcher.

The Lillian Goldman Reading Room.

Finally, we went to the reading room itself—a glittering room with a circulation center at one end and three walls filled with books on two floors. With a total collection of 500,000 volumes, the vast majority of the Center's holdings are in closed stacks. They also claim to own 100,000,000 documents. Until recently, they had relied on paper forms for patrons to request materials, but now they have gone to an electronic format powered by Aeon Software to facilitate access to their collections for researchers.

LIBRARY: POETS HOUSE

Address: 10 River Terrace (at Murray Street), New York, NY 10282
URL: http://www.poetshouse.org/
Telephone: (212) 431-7920
E-mail: info@poetshouse.org
Access: Open to the public

Facebook: https://www.facebook.com/poetshouse
Twitter: https://twitter.com/poetshouse
Transportation: Subway–Chambers Street Station of #1, 2 or 3 lines

It is a system that did not make me very happy—sometimes I would send an e-mail to a library or fill out a contact form and never hear back. This was the case here, but since I was already in Lower Manhattan for another visit, I decided to stop by and announce myself, hoping to make an appointment for a future visit. In this case, I was greeted by their Public Relations Director Suzanne Lunden, who graciously gave me a thorough tour on the spot.

Poets House is in a gleaming apartment high rise in Battery Park City. I had the vague idea that (given the location) this was started by well-heeled art lovers in Manhattan, but I could not have been more wrong about that. The organization was started in SoHo in 1985 by two-time Poet Laureate Stanley Kunitz and others in a grass-roots movement with big dreams and little money. Kunitz died in 2006 at the age of 100. (Am I the only one who notes that composers and comedians such as George Burns, Eubie Blake, and Bob Hope live to 100 while great athletes never do?) Cofounder Elizabeth Kray started the reading series at the library. In a fierce competition they won a grant from the developer to get their prime space rent-free, and they opened there in 2010.

The collection holds 60,000 volumes, all of which are noncirculating. I tried to stump them with my favorite Chinese poet Li Po, but they had several volumes in the P section. Also, a favorite book from my graduate school days, *Groceries*, by Herbert Scott, was on the shelves. Lunden told me that all of the books are donated by publishers. Their downstairs area has a comfortable meeting room area, which holds many poetry readings and lectures. It opens to a boulder-strewn section of park between the large buildings, and in the milder months, they open it up and do programs in an amphitheater carved just outside their door. Lunden also said that the library hosts a Brooklyn Bridge walk in June, in which people walk across the span in a group and stop for poetry readings along the way.

Display case with poet memorabilia.

As we walked up the stairs, I looked into a spacious glass display room over-looking the Hudson River. It was winter, and the display included hand-painted holiday greeting cards from famous poets. Moving on to the stack area, one noticed that the library was enthusiastically attended by a mostly young crowd. Lunden told me that their user base was about half people with an interest in poetry and half people who used the space for study and Wi-Fi. Famous users of the library have included numerous poet laureates of the United States. Past the stacks there is a special area for chapbooks—independently published pamphlet-sized works from still-unknown poets. They also collect items from the "Mimeo Revolution," which predated that much larger Internet Revolution.

Famous poet portraits in a quiet research room.

Beyond the chapbooks there is an audiovisual area, with CD readings and even a record collection, which had attracted good press in the local media recently. "We have to check out the needles separately with a driver's license, or people will steal them," Lunden told me. Then there is a piece of furniture that may well be their flagship holding. A writing desk owned by E. E. Cummings was donated to the library in 2011.

LIBRARY: HISPANIC SOCIETY OF AMERICA

Address: 613 West 155th Street, New York, NY 10032
URL: http://www.hispanicsociety.org/hispanic/library.htm
Telephone: (212) 926-2234
E-mail: http://www.hispanicsociety.org/hispanic/forms/frmRare-Books.htm
Access: Open to the public
Facebook: https://www.facebook.com/pages/Hispanic-Society-of-America/112373672107403?fref=ts
Transportation: Subway – #1 line to 157th Street

It has often been the case in this project that I get the best leads from other libraries that I visit. This was true with the Hispanic Society Library, which I was completely unaware of when I established my list of target libraries. When I was visiting the Cervantes Institute library late in my game I was asked about the Hispanic. "You have to see them if at all possible. They have things like a first edition of Don Quixote," I was told. I did some research and found out that this was all true. A phone call established that they would happily participate in this book, so a time was set on a spring Friday.

When I got out of the station I was in a section of Manhattan that I never knew existed. It was a bustling shopping street with plenty of options to eat or drink. The campus was two blocks to the south and across the street. Inside a giant marble courtyard there is Boricua College on the right and the Hispanic Society on the left. I entered and walked past a series of objects that transported me to the Middle Ages. A great wooden door at the end of the room led to the library. Walking past a card catalog on either side I went ahead to the reference desk and announced myself.

A middle-aged man in jeans and T-shirt emerged from the back room and announced himself as John O'Neill. Judging by his general appearance and accent, he was not, himself, Hispanic. He was, it turned out, a scholar with a Ph.D. in medieval studies. I asked him which county he hailed from, and the answer was Londonderry.

"There are 15,000 books here printed before 1701, and 250 of them are incunabula," O'Neill said. There are also 150,000+ more modern titles and the holdings include 50,000 periodicals. The library was an important part of the enterprise in the early days. "In 20 years Huntington built this into a world-class library." The arrangement is a combination of Dewey, Library of Congress, and homemade classification. Manuscripts are filed in accession number order. The library's collection is still not described in an online catalog, but they are working to fix that eventually.

The building itself is quite historic. It was on farmland purchased by Archer Milton Huntington for this purpose. He created a magnificent beaux arts Audubon Terrace complex in 1904. In addition to the Hispanic Society, the complex also housed the Museum of the American Indian and the Numismatic Society before both relocated later to Lower Manhattan.

The reading room is particularly magnificent, with dark shelves surrounded by sculpture and paintings. On the left side of the room there is an embroidered map of the world from 1526. O'Neill risked life and limb to clear the curtains away so I could get a good shot of the work. The library is best known for its Cervantes and *Quixote* editions, but I suspect that this is the most valuable holding.

A 1526 embroidery of a map of the world.

The library's manuscript collection contains more than 300 documents signed by Spanish kings. The charter of the library says that it will cover all areas where Spanish is spoken, going as far as the Philippines, but clearly, looking at the artwork and other evidence, the emphasis is on Spain.

The main reading room of the library.

I asked O'Neill how Huntington came by his passion for Hispanic culture and was told that this would remain a mystery. He did travel to Spain as a young man and also spent some time on a ranch in Texas. Could there have been some sort of romantic entanglement that led to this passion? It appears that we will never know.

As always, I asked O'Neill about which famous persons had been into the library. The first answer was the royal family of Spain. Also, the presidents of the Dominican Republic and the European Union had visited. Closer to home, Tony Bennett had been by to see the *Don Quixote* first edition. If any of them had asked where to go for lunch, he would have probably pointed out the Salvadorean restaurant on 156th Street, although the restaurant might have been a bit bewildered in the matter of feeding a king and his queen.

LIBRARY: NEW YORK CITY NEW YORK
FAMILY HISTORY CENTER

Address: 125 Columbus Avenue, First Floor, New York, NY 10023
URL: https://familysearch.org/learn/wiki/en/New_York_City_New_York_Family_History_Center
Telephone: (212) 799-2414
E-mail: NY_NewYorkCity@ldsmail.net
Access: Open to the public

"Are you aware of the Latter Day Saints?" asked the woman who was managing the library. I explained to her that I grew up in Phoenix and had considerable knowledge about the church. In Arizona, it is a very common sight to find Mormon missionaries riding their bikes with their white shirts and black name tags. As someone who has used Familysearch.org considerably for years, and has visited the main library facility in Salt Lake City, I also have tremendous respect for what they have accomplished. The library is located in a prime Midtown area across the street from Lincoln Center, and the building itself is eye-catching. I was there to see the New York Public Library performing arts branch and had a bit of time on my hands before they opened, so I dropped in on the Latter Day Saints library one morning in winter.

The public room (which was all I saw that day) is entirely computerized now, although I understand that they still have a considerable collection of microform data farther into the building. The librarian on duty, named Sister Hansen, was very informative. She told me that it is their belief that in the afterlife we will all live with our families, so it is a good investment to learn as much about our family trees as possible. These facilities are a way of getting people to think about their ancestors. In her case, she said that she has traced her family tree all the way back to Adam and Eve. I was somewhat startled to hear this, and admit that I chuckled briefly. If this was true then she certainly did not need any further work on her own personal family tree, so it is appropriate for her to help others with theirs.

In addition to the main facility at Salt Lake City, there are 15 major research centers in the country. As big as the New York City operation is, it is not counted as one of the 15.

Other researchers arrived when I was talking to her, so I had to cut my visit short, but she did send me on my way with a substantial amount of information.

LIBRARY: AMERICAN KENNEL CLUB

Address: 260 Madison Avenue, New York, NY 10016
URL: http://www.akc.org/about/departments/
Telephone: (212) 696-8200
E-mail: https://www.apps.akc.org/apps/contact/index.cfm
Access: Open to the public
Facebook: https://www.facebook.com/AmericanKennelClub?fref=ts
Twitter: @akcdoglovers

Introduction: The dog library is the catalyst for this entire book, so I went into this visit with a feeling of high expectation. Adding to that personal connection, I have been a dog owner for almost 40 years, even though there have been only three dogs in that time.

I visited the American Kennel Club library in early spring, on a day when I would go on to visit the American Museum of Natural History, so it was a very dense day. Across the street I saw my first tulips of the year. This building is one of those high rises for which you have to get a pass from Security to go up the elevator, but the atmosphere here was fairly relaxed. Getting off the elevator, you are immediately immersed in the universe of dogs. There were dog trophies, dog sculptures, and dog paintings, and that was before you actually walked into the club.

A crystalline dog sculpture that needs to be seen from all angles.

I met archivist Craig Savino at the main reference desk. When you approach the desk it is hard to keep your eyes off the giant crystal sculpture with images of dogs floating in it, so that you see various breeds as you circle the piece. Behind the desk there is a mirrored display cabinet with enormous silver trophies from past events. As I took note of the breeds, I could not escape the irony that some of the trophies were bigger than the animal being honored.

Some of the trophies held by the library.

Savino began showing me the specifics of the library. In the southern half of the room there are the general categories such as sporting dogs—analogous to the categories you would find at the Westminster Dog Show.

Paintings showing howe the Jack Russell terrier changed over a few centuries.

Beyond that, the books are alphabetized by specific breed. Farther down, you find show catalogs—so many of them that the library had to install compact shelving. Many libraries complain that the Dewey and Library of Congress schemes do not work well in a library that contains very specific subject matter, but most adapt the major schemes, so it was interesting to visit a library that used an entirely original plan, though they did have limited use of Dewey in their rare books section.

Book plate from the library's early days.

Savino said that there are more than 170 recognized breeds in the organization. More information can be found in their newest edition of *The Complete
Dog Book*, which has not been published for a decade. I was surprised about this,
since the dog book has been a staple in my entire library career, and I just
assumed that they published it every year, like the *Guinness World Records*.

First edition of "Dogs in America."

On the north side of the room there are the stud books going back to the late 1880s. Also there are bench show field trials and books of records and standards for breeds. The American Kennel Club was founded in 1884, following the merger of 10 American and three Canadian kennel clubs. J.M. Taylor was their first president. With so much history here, it seems like a natural thing to digitize. Savino told me that they have worked with digitizing archival material, but not much with books. Given that so much has been done in the public domain area by Google and Internet Archive, this is probably pretty sensible. They do have a service to create PDF files on demand.

The west wall contains their rarest items in a glass case. One of the most significant books I was shown was titled *Ten Thousand Miles with a Dog Sled*.

I didn't know that dogs existed 30 million years ago, but here is the fossil.

I asked where they send people when asked for restaurant recommendations, and Savino told me that he personally prefers the falafel cart on 5th Avenue and 39th Street. For a splurge, he likes the restaurant named Shakespeare around the corner.

The library prides itself on being the place for one-stop shopping for anything you would ever want to know about dogs. Justifiably so.

LIBRARY: CHANCELLOR ROBERT R. LIVINGSTON MASONIC LIBRARY

Address: 71 West 23rd Street, No. 1400
URL: http://www.nymasoniclibrary.org/
Telephone: (212) 337-6620
E-mail: info@nymasoniclibrary.org
Access: Open to the public
Facebook: https://www.facebook.com/pages/The-Chancellor-Robert-R-Livingston-Masonic-Library/11066400895323

This visit was unusually personal to me. My dad was a Mason and Shriner for many decades and a past Master of his lodge in Mesa, Arizona. I never heard him say it, but it must have been disappointing that neither of his sons joined. Even though I did not follow in his footsteps, I saw the way that his involvement enhanced his life, so I have always had the greatest respect for the Order. The library stood out when I was searching for places to include in this book. Given that the Masons are a secret organization, how do they treat nonmembers coming in to look at their books? How do they cope with an age in which all information is available online for anyone who really wants to find out?

When the day came, I went to the 14th floor, after passing a bust of Will Rogers (again calling to mind my father, who was a huge admirer). Once up the elevator I entered a library that just glowed with ornate charm—lots of stained glass and impressive artwork. I was met by library director Tom Savini. He told me that the library contained 60,000 volumes, covering World Masonry in all of its flavors. Since there is no absolute governing body, some of the variations can be a real departure from Masonry as it is best known.

One of the library's attractive display cases.

We went into Tom's office, where my eye was drawn to a bust of Theodore Roosevelt, who seemed to be almost everywhere in these visits. He told me he had joined the Masons because he loved history, and he admired their record for religious tolerance. He told me that the building dates back to 1910 and that it initially contained 12 lodge meeting rooms and an auditorium. The latter has been a good source of revenue over the years, as by now the building is only half taken up by the Masons.

The library concentrates on New York State lodges, but its holdings go considerably beyond our state. With all of the old and scarce materials here, digitization would seem like a natural thing to pursue, and Savini said that they have been aggressively doing that since 2013. Manuscript holdings of lodges are very important for this process.

Heading to the stacks, Tom introduced me to his library staff, including a cataloger and a young man who ran the Canon-based digitization station. They began asking me about which libraries I was covering, and I was given a long list of places that had not been on my list. On further investigation, most of them were museums with no libraries, but one was The Players Club, which turned out to be a very promising lead, and I am eternally grateful.

The library has roots that go well beyond the construction of the current building. A library committee was formed in 1855, and a major book collection was procured a decade later. Savini says that there is a Scottish Rites library in Lexington, Massachusetts, but keep in mind that Scottish Rites are not considered to be a pure form of Masonry, but a group that builds on the original.

As always, I asked who is the most famous person who has used the library, and the answer was Tommy Lee, the drummer for Motley Crue, as well as Congressman John Brademas. Otherwise, the library's users are 50% practicing Masons, with the other half being curious family members like myself.

Savini showing one of his oldest books.

Savini took me back into the large stack area and talked about how hard it is to make decisions for information technology that will last the ages. Ten years ago, it seemed a pretty safe bet that CD-ROMs and DVDs would be the future, but now the game has moved on into the Cloud.

LIBRARY: SCHOMBURG CENTER FOR RESEARCH IN BLACK CULTURE

Address: 515 Malcolm X Blvd, New York, NY
URL: http://www.nypl.org/locations/schomburg
Telephone: (917) 275-6975
E-mail: http://www.nypl.org/help/email-a-librarian/JBH-research-and-reference-division
Access: Open to the public
Facebook: https://www.facebook.com/pages/Schomburg-Center/150438445005908?fref=ts
Twitter: https://twitter.com/SchomburgCenter
Transportation: Subway – 2 or 3 line to 135th Street

Since I began working for the College of New Rochelle, I have had several opportunities to visit our library's branch on 125th Street in Harlem. I have found this to be a vibrant and exciting community. Importantly, it is full of excellent restaurants, and I have already developed a favorites list. What I had never done is visit the Schomburg, although it was on my list of libraries to visit from the very first. Because I never got permission to talk to the authorities there, I went to my usual plan B. I visited the library as a card-carrying New York Public Library patron and will simply report what I saw.

Nobody bothered me when I explored the various floors carrying my briefcase, but when I decided to see the manuscripts and rare books room, I abided by the rules, went down to the first floor, and checked my bag. The room was filled with art, sculpture, and display cases with documents concerning the Antigua and Barbuda Progressive Society in the 1940s. People who need copies of books or documents have the option of using a Minolta book-friendly scanner.

I did not visit the photograph room, although I understand that they own 11,000,000 prints. I did find someone who I will refer to as "Unnamed Source" who answered a few questions about the library. I was told that Harry Belafonte and Wynton Marsalis had been in. For lunch recommendations, Unnamed Source mentioned that the building across the street had a cafeteria. Also Jacob's Hot and Cold Buffet, International House of Pancakes, and a food truck that was parked outside the library door. For significant holding, I was referred to a book called GOAT, for *Greatest of All Time*, meaning Muhammad Ali.

LIBRARY: LESBIAN HERSTORY ARCHIVES

Address: 484 14th Street, Brooklyn, NY 11215
Phone: (718) 768-3953
Access: Open to the public
URL: lesbianherstoryarchives.org
Facebook: facebook.com/pages/Lesbian-Herstory-Archives/
24939682269?fref=ts
Transportation: Subway: 2, 3 Eastern Parkway, bus, #37 from Atlantic
Avenue Terminal

My visit to the Lesbian Herstory Archives was due entirely to chance. One day late in the project I happened to be looking at Google Maps to get the location of the Brooklyn Botanical Garden. I noticed the Lesbian Herstory Archive just blocks away. I checked their Web page and found that they were open to the public during the limited hours of operation, so I gave them a call and found that they were delighted to be included in my book. I was equally delighted because this represents the kind of diversity that I was after.

I scheduled my visit for late on a Friday after talking to the Botanical Garden representative and was reminded that things can look close on the map but still be a bit of a hike in real life. If I were going there again, I would take the bus down from Atlantic Avenue. Once I got to the address, I found myself in a quiet residential neighborhood just off of Prospect Park. I rang the buzzer and was greeted by Kayleigh, a young woman who has worked in the archive for two years while studying library science nearby and also holding down a paraprofessional job in a Manhattan university library.

I was led into a living room filled with file cabinets and shelves packed ceiling high with books. At the end of the room there was a comfortable couch in front of the window facing 14th Street. Kayleigh told me that the library contained 14,000 volumes in addition to a substantial collection of files on historical figures in their cause. The library also includes 1300 periodical titles. I was told that the library had a staff of 11, all of them volunteers. I was surprised to learn that the archives have been in existence since

1974, when they were created by members of the Gay Academic Union, a community on the Upper West Side, who were mainly academics at City University of New York colleges in the area. The archives have been at their current location since 1993. Before that, the archives were located in the apartment of cofounder Joan Nestle.

I was well aware during our talk that I was not exactly their average visitor, but the exchange of information went very smoothly. The only thing that made me uncomfortable was her use of the term "Queer studies." When I was growing up, this would have been considered a derogatory term, but we all know that situations change with time. I was told that the archives maintain an active schedule of programs, including readings, speed dating, and film screenings.

The library's holdings cover a variety of genres, including humor, comics, science fiction, juvenile, and young adult. A separate collection of titles donated by the Daughters of Bilitis is maintained at the archives.

In response to my standard question about which famous person had used the library, there was a moment's hesitation, because some of the users may not wish to be identified, but soon she pointed out the feminist poet Adrienne Rich as a library user. Another standard question is where to send people who want a good lunch. The first name that came up was Ladybird Bakery. Honorable mention went to Terrace Bagels and Connecticut Muffins.

FURTHER READING

American Sephardi Federation: http://www.sephardi.house/.
Antigua and Barbuda Progressive Society: http://www.abpsociety.org/.
Article on the Poet's House as a study space: http://nyulocal.com/on-campus/2011/11/10/nyc-tip-poets-house-on-the-hudson-is-a-great-place-to-study-1/.
Biography of Elizabeth Kray: http://www.poets.org/poetsorg/poet/elizabeth-kray/.
Biography of Stanley Kunitz: http://www.poets.org/poetsorg/poet/stanley-kunitz.
Biography of Tommy Lee: http://www.biography.com/people/tommy-lee-222294.
American Jewish Historical Society: http://www.ajhs.org/.
Cahnman Preservation wing: http://www.cjh.org/p/140.
CBS article about poetry readings in New York: http://newyork.cbslocal.com/guide/5-best-venues-for-spoken-word-and-poetry-readings-in-new-york/.
Center for Jewish History Decade of distinction: http://www.cjh.org/cjh_today/2011_decade.pdf.
John Brademas in Wikipedia: http://en.wikipedia.org/wiki/John_Brademas.
Leo Baeck Institute: http://www.lbi.org/.
Nearby restaurants to the Center for Jewish History: http://www.tripadvisor.com/RestaurantsNear-g60763-d528121-Center_for_Jewish_History-New_York_City_New_York.html.

Wall Street Journal article about the AKC library: http://en.wikipedia.org/wiki/American_Kennel_Club.

Wikipedia article about the Poet's House: http://en.wikipedia.org/wiki/Poets_House.

Wikipedia article about the Family History Centers: https://en.wikipedia.org/wiki/Family_History_Center_(LDS_Church).

Wikipedia article on American Kennel Club Library: http://en.wikipedia.org/wiki/American_Kennel_Club.

Yelp review of the Poet's House: http://www.yelp.com/biz/poets-house-new-york.

Yelp review of the Schomburg Library: http://www.yelp.com/biz/schomburg-center-for-research-in-black-culture-new-york-3.

Yeshiva University Museum: http://www.yumuseum.org/.

Yivo Institute for Jewish Research: http://www.yivo.org/.

CHAPTER 14

History

We learn from history that we've learned nothing from history.

George Bernard Shaw

LIBRARY: AMERICAN IRISH HISTORICAL SOCIETY

Address: 991 5th Avenue, New York, NY 10028
URL: http://aihs.org/
Telephone: (212) 288-2263
E-mail: http://aihs.org/contact/
Access: Open to researchers by appointment
Facebook:https://www.facebook.com/pages/American-Irish-Historical-Society/187462474615362
Bus access: M70 crosstown bus or the M4 south on 5th Avenue; also the M3/4 bus north on Madison Avenue

I have more than a passing, academic interest in Irish history. During my time as a systems librarian at Quinnipiac University, I managed to get involved in the university's projects in the study of the Irish famine, and I was rewarded with four school-sponsored trips to the west of Ireland. In those visits, I managed to set up a program to digitize actual handwritten pages from the Board of Guardians Minute Books in Killarney and Kenmare, detailing the attempts of authorities to deal with a country that was falling apart owing to crop failures.

In my Quinnipiac years I made one trip to the American Irish Historical Society (AIHS) in its posh 5th Avenue headquarters, so I knew that the society had a substantial collection that would be of interest to any Irish history researcher. In the late winter of 2015, I visited the site again and spent an hour with William Hurley. A soft-spoken but energetic young man, he impressed me immediately with his technical expertise. Like many of the special libraries, AIHS maintained a catalog using Koha. Unlike everybody else, Hurley was proficient enough in ILS technology to run the catalog without any sort of help from the Koha facilitation companies.

50 Specialty Libraries of New York City
ISBN 978-0-08-100554-5

As we walked through the many floors of the old mansion, Hurley told me that this was originally a gracious private home, built in 1900, and upgraded by the famous architect and designer Ogden Codman, Jr. Hurley told me that there are more than 12,000 cataloged books in the collection, and a large archive of magazines and newspapers, with the main focus being the Irish immigrant experience in New York. That collection includes the world's only known full set of *The Gaelic American* from the 1880s. From 1898 to 1942, the society published the *Journal of the American Irish Historical Society*. There is also a substantial collection of Fenian pamphlets from the nineteenth century. As we walked through the various floors, I saw a lot of sports trophies, as the new Americans gravitated to team sports.

The parent organization has been around since 1897, and its members have included notables such as Theodore Roosevelt and George M. Cohan. One of the parlors sports a giant painting of Roosevelt (one of 50 founding members), who I would also see later at the Masonic library. The Society is nonsectarian and nonpartisan and exists only to shine a light on the Irish American experience.

Hurley showed me a group of scrapbooks containing newspaper and magazine clippings of Irish American interest, but admitted that the contents, while valuable, do not contain citations, so it is hard to place them in any specific context. The *real* prize in the archive area was a large collection of dictation tapes containing the voice of Brendan Behan, who had no use for a typewriter. This gets the AIHS a lot of attention, but copyright concerns limit the use of this collection.

The major collection of book titles was found in the basement. With its compact shelves and nonambient lighting, it was clearly designed for staff use and not researcher visits. I saw a variety of books, including Irish language and travel books, but the main focus is history. There is also a fairly substantial collection of Catholic history. Most books are in English, but there are many Irish language works. "Books in Gaelic are harder to digitize and OCR," said Hurley.

At the end of the tour, I was shown the book digitization area. The machine we used at Quinnipiac cost more than $30,000, but Hurley was able to build his only book-friendly scanning machine and outfit it with digital cameras that were programmed in-house. The OCR, or optical character recognition, program they used was FineReader, which is the program we had relied on at Quinnipiac.

As I walked out of the elegant foyer and onto 5th Avenue, I could not help thinking, whoever is watching the St. Patrick's day parade from those upper floors truly has the luck of the Irish.

LIBRARY: OTHMER LIBRARY—BROOKLYN HISTORICAL SOCIETY

Address: 128 Pierrepont Street, Brooklyn, NY 11201
URL: http://www.brooklynhistory.org/library/about.html
Telephone: (718) 222-4111
E-mail: library@brooklynhistory.org
Access: Open to the public
Facebook: https://www.facebook.com/BrooklynHistory?fref=ts
Blog: http://www.brooklynhistory.org/blog/

When we first moved to New York, we were eager to explore all the sections of the city, so it was not long before I took the family down to Coney Island to see the aquarium and the theme park. To a recently arrived family of Arizonans, Brooklyn held a special place in the mythology of our new city. Furthermore, my family records show a deep connection to Brooklyn, where my grandmother grew up and married a man who had just arrived from Texas to serve in the Navy. I was very happy to find out that the librarians could talk to me on fairly short notice.

One of many quiet corners in the library's research area.

The building is a wonder in itself. It was built in 1881 as the Long Island Historical Society. Even though Brooklyn was adopted by New York City in the late nineteenth century, they did not change the name until 1985. I was met by reference librarian Joanna Lamaida. She told me that the library owns 33,000 books, 1600 archival collections, 1200 oral history interviews, 50,000 photographs, 8000 artifacts, 300 paintings, and 2000 maps, which document the commercial, residential, community, and civic development of the borough. Of all this, it was hard for them to name one thing that they considered the flagship item, but they had several major contenders, including a copy of the Emancipation Proclamation and a Bernard Ratzer map showing the positions of George Washington's troops at the Battle of Brooklyn.

Research corner displaying one of the library's 50,000 photographs.

The building is notable in several ways. Many of the libraries in this book are more than 100 years old, but this is one of the very few still operating out of its original building. I was told that the construction was an architectural innovation for the time, with columns not in the center of the room, creating a wide open space. They told me that the construction was partially inspired by the Brooklyn Bridge. I asked how the building fared during Hurricane Sandy and was told that they came through unscathed. "We had a few days where we had to close, and lots of our staff people used the time to go out and volunteer with the cleanup effort," said Julie May. That is Brooklyn Pride.

They are heavily into social media, with accounts on all of the major players, as well as a library blog. They are involved in the Brooklyn Digital Heritage Project along with the Brooklyn Museum and the Brooklyn Public Library. They also partner with New York University (NYU) for their online catalog and work with NYU's archivist program to host interns.

Their users are a mixed group of neighborhood people needing a quiet place to study, people needing help with landmark status for their properties, tourists, and genealogists. Whether they are museum members or not, all of the collections are noncirculating.

Going out the door on my way to the Brooklyn Botanical Garden, I was reminded of the signs that we used to see on the Belt Parkway while headed East—"You are now leaving Brooklyn. Fuggetaboutit."

LIBRARY: BRONX HISTORICAL SOCIETY

Address: Bronx County Historical Society, 3309 Bainbridge Avenue, The Bronx, NY 10467
URL: http://www.bronxhistoricalsociety.org/library
Telephone: (718) 881-8900
E-mail: librarian@bronxhistoricalsociety.org
Access: Open to the public—note limited hours
Facebook: https://www.facebook.com/pages/Bronx-Historical-Society/115554328467463?fref=ts
Transportation: Subway line D to 205th Street

There is a wonderful line in the movie *Awakenings*, in which Robert De Niro is playing a patient who has revived after decades of being in a coma. His doctor, played by Robin Williams, is driving him to the beach in the Bronx. "What a beautiful place the Bronx has become!" exclaims De Niro. We saw this in the theaters when it came out, and we gave this a hearty laugh, even though we were regular Bronx visitors. Those visits were due to several things. First, there is the Bronx Zoo, which is one of the wonders of New York. Second, there is a baseball team in the Bronx that has given us many happy moments. Third, there is City Island, a relatively unknown strip of land in Long Island Sound that delivers the best seafood in all of New York.

I wrote to Laura Tosi, librarian at the Bronx County Historical Society, and set up an appointment on a Wednesday afternoon, to follow my visit to the New York Botanical Garden. My plan was to catch a cab and make my way up the two miles that separated the libraries. I then got a lesson in Outer Borough cab service. The taxi we reserved simply never showed up, so I had to postpone my visit. Next time, I took the subway from Penn Station to 205th Street (Laura had warned me that parking near their facility was the impossible dream). When I got out, I was surprised to learn that I had to walk only two short blocks to see the library, which was housed in a brownstone building across the street from the main museum. The library was started in the late 1960s and moved out of the museum into its current quarters in 1980. The library owns 25,000 books and 35,000 historic photographs.

The main reading room.

The main reading room is divided, with New York State and City books on the right and Bronx-only books on the left. The first are in Library of Congress order, and the second use a homemade classification scheme. They do not have a publicly accessible online catalog, but their card catalog has been replaced with a program called FileMaker Pro, which is available to the library staff. They are particularly proud of their photograph collection. Other significant holdings include *The Bronx Home News*, which is available on microfilm for the years 1907–1948. There are city directories from 1927 to the 1970s and in paper after that. This kind of material gets them attention from genealogy researchers around the world.

One of the library's many historic photographs.

The library is funded by the city and the state, as well as by memberships. It has no regular digitization program yet, but it does offer digitization on demand for patrons who need a JPEG of their materials. For lunch suggestions, they send people to Sal's Pizzeria down the street and to the coffee shop next to the subway station.

LIBRARY: STATEN ISLAND MUSEUM

Address: 75 Stuyvesant Place, Staten Island, NY 10301
Telephone: (718) 483-7122
URL: StatenIslandMuseum.org

Staten Island was famous in this project for being the toughest borough to cover. There was a really cool-sounding institution called the Staten Island Tools Library for citizens who were recovering from Super Storm Sandy, but they had no access but a Web page, so when they ignored my message, there was no fallback. I was happy to find the Staten Island Museum for two reasons. First because it assured coverage of five boroughs. Second, they are located at Snug Harbor, which is one of my favorite places in the city.

This was one of only two libraries for which my visit did not involve public transportation. While it was technically possible to take the Long Island

Railroad, the No. 1 subway, the Staten Island ferry, and then a bus to Snug Harbor, that would have involved a day of travel that I could not afford. I took the first exit from the Verrazano Bridge and headed south on what Google assured me was a main road. I finally made it to Snug Harbor with a minute to spare.

A historic map of Staten Island.

I met Cara Dellatte, the archivist in her office, which overlooked the garden, at the beginning of spring. I found that the library is one more for the 100-year club, having been founded in 1881, and the original library was entirely devoted to science. At this time, the museum had already been in existence for 50 years. It was created with a partnership including the city and private nonprofit interests. It has been at its current location since 2009, and Dellatte believes that they will remain for some time. She has been with the museum for nearly 10 years, first as an intern and then being promoted to archivist in 2010.

The collection is not indexed by an online catalog, so inquiries from researchers are handled by the archival staff using a card catalog. The collection is filed in Dewey order. They are currently not working with OCLC to display their holdings in WorldCat, although it is on their wish list to change that. The archive is used by genealogists, authors, and students. They also handle many internal requests from the Museum.

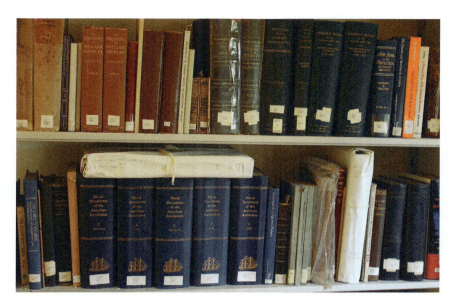

A peek inside of the locked book cabinets at Snug Harbor.

I asked Cara what she considered to be her flagship holding. I was told that Dellatte had discovered a small book sitting in a stack of things for evaluation that turned out to be a gold mine. It was a pencil-written diary of life on the island from 1861 to 1866 that gave a glimpse of northern life in the Civil War and immediately afterward.

The archive also contains documents signed by British General William Howe during the Revolutionary War. Also there is a collection of letters to home from local soldiers during the Civil War. Their oldest holdings include English land grants from as far back as 1605.

FURTHER READING

An American Family grows up in Brooklyn: http://www.brooklynhistory.org/exhibitions/lefferts/.

Brooklyn Historical Society Library blog: http://www.brooklynhistory.org/blog/.

Brooklyn Visual Heritage: http://www.brooklynvisualheritage.org/.

Brooklyn Waterfront history: http://www.brooklynwaterfronthistory.org/.

Brooklyn's Antislavery movement: http://pursuitoffreedom.org/.

Irish Central news story about the 5th Avenue building: http://www.irishcentral.com/roots/genealogy/Who-lived-in-the-spectacular-American-Irish-Historical-Society-building.html#.

Irish History Digitized: http://www.greathunger.org.

Wikipedia entry for The American Irish American Society: http://en.wikipedia.org/wiki/American_Irish_Historical_Society.

Wikipedia entry for Wolfe Tone http://en.wikipedia.org/wiki/Wolfe_Tone.

CHAPTER 15

Botany and Horticulture

Flowers always make people better, happier, and more helpful; they are
sunshine, food, and medicine for the soul.

Luther Burbank

LIBRARY: BROOKLYN BOTANICAL GARDENS LIBRARY

Address: 1000 Washington Avenue, Brooklyn, NY
URL: http://www.bbg.org/research/library
Telephone: (718) 623-7200
E-mail: library@bbg.org
Access: Open to the public
Twitter: https://twitter.com/bklynbotanic

I have been a patron of the Brooklyn Botanical Gardens since the
early 1990s, but it was not until 2012 that I knew they had a library. We
were at the Gardens for a weekend visit in the spring for the Cherry
Blossom Festival and found the library by accident. With its semicircular
interior ranges built around a rotunda, I thought it to be a perfect gem
of a library. Marble statues of great scientists line the top floor, staring
down at library users.

50 Specialty Libraries of New York City
ISBN 978-0-08-100554-5

Public stack area of the library.

I met with librarian Kathy Crosby in the spring of 2015 to revisit the library and get a sense of where it is headed. She warned me in advance that the library is going through a restructuring of materials, so things might be messy. With my deadline looming, I decided to risk it. I arrived with a minimum of trouble and met with Ms. Crosby in her office, located around the corner from the book stacks.

The library is full of imaginative display pieces.

I soon learned that Brooklyn Botanical is in that fairly large group of libraries that have been operating for more than 100 years. They started in 1910 with a collection of four books. Despite the compact appearance of the library, that number has now grown to over 80,000. There are also more than 200,000 archival items, such as lantern slides, negatives, and institutional papers.

Current periodical display.

With all of these older items, it was a natural thing to ask about digitization, but so far they have done none of their own, although they do provide access to other online books. So far they have been using Library of Congress classification, but they may modify that in the future to make it work better for their own specialty. The books are indexed in a SydneyPLUS integrated library system, which I am told is a popular choice for special libraries. I tried searching the catalog for a subject that seemed surefire: the gardens at Monticello. I got 13 hits, and seven of them displayed color images of book covers, so the catalog looked efficient and appealing.

When asked about famous visitors, the name that came up right away was E. O. Wilson.

LIBRARY: THE BARBARA A. MARGOLIS LIBRARY OF THE HORTICULTURAL SOCIETY OF NEW YORK

Address: 148 West 37th Street, New York, NY 10018
URL: https://thehort.org/education_library.html
Telephone: (212) 757-0915
E-mail: info@thehort.org
Access: Open to the public on weekdays
Facebook: https://www.facebook.com/thehortnyc?fref=ts

My only connection to horticulture is that I am married to a woman with a green thumb. Donna can make almost anything grow, although we hit a brick wall last year when we tried to plant zucchini in a spot that used to contain a tree before Hurricane Sandy. I, on the other hand, have a rock garden out back on a spot of land that would never grow grass.

I was scheduled to meet Sara Hobel, and I arrived early, so I had a chance to browse through the library for a few minutes. I noted that the books were overwhelmingly large pictorial volumes and that they were arranged in Library of Congress order. I soon found the rock garden section and found out something that I never knew—if I want to go to the absolute Mecca for Zen gardens, I must plan a visit to the Japanese city of Kyoto.

When Sara met me, I asked her which book in the library she considered to be the flagship holding, and I was told that they owned a copy of Philip Miller's seminal work, *The Dictionary of Gardening*. She told me that whatever the political differences between England and America, there was good synergy among the gardening enthusiasts, so lots of seeds and shoots made their way across the Atlantic in both directions. Another significant holding is a book about the naturalist John Bartram by Andrea Wulf. Unfortunately, there is no online catalog to make advance plans to see a book. On the other hand, this is a substantial library, so whatever your interest in horticulture, they are likely to have books about it.

The library is funded entirely by the parent organization. It was originally started as a pet project of one of the Frick daughters in the early twentieth century. The library is multipurpose, and the space is often used for programs, as it was on the day I visited.

Special collections include their Botanical Illustration Collection, popular with artists and others who appreciate finely produced books about plants. The American Landscape History Collection supports research on gardening in America during the late nineteenth and early twentieth centuries. The History of American Horticulture Collection contains practical books and magazines from 1850 to 1950. They also maintain an archive of institutional records.

LIBRARY: THE LUESTHER T. MERTZ LIBRARY, NEW YORK BOTANICAL GARDENS

Address: 2900 Southern Blvd, Bronx, NY 10458
URL: http://www.nybg.org/library/
Telephone: (718) 817-8700
E-mail: libref@nybg.org
Access: Open to the public with Garden admission; circulation privileges for members
Transportation: Metro North Botanical Garden Station

There are two shining cultural institutions in the Bronx (three if you count the New York Yankees), and I will confess that in my time as a New Yorker I have made more trips to the New York Zoological Society (at one point I believe they gave up and just went back to calling it the Bronx Zoo because everyone else does). Across the Pelham Parkway is the New York Botanical Gardens. We went there in the early 1990s, and then about 10 years later for an unforgettable wedding. When it came time to write this book, the Botanical Gardens had a major advantage— it has a library that is demonstrably world class. When I contacted the library I was given an appointment with Stephen Sinon, Head of Archives.

The compact shelving room gives a hint of the enormity of this collection.

One thing that stands out immediately is that he is enormously proud of this library. I mentioned hearing that it was the largest such library in America. "Not so," he said. "The largest in the world." I learned that their book collection contains more than half a million volumes. One book hails from the late twelfth century—the earliest known copy of a ninth century book of Greco-Roman and Arabic plant knowledge. There are 14,000 journal titles, some going back to the seventeenth century.

The library allows some book circulation to garden members.

I always ask about which famous people have used the library. Sinon's answer sounded like the opening of the Academy Awards—Sigourney Weaver, Daniel Day Lewis, and Helen Mirren. Authors Oliver Sacks and E.O. Wilson have used the library, as have members of the British royal family. Two television series have been filmed here in recent years. On the shelves opposite the reference desk I saw a picture of Michelle Obama and asked if she had been in. The answer was no, but she had invited them to the White House to collect an award.

The library keeps track of its holdings in an Innovative Interfaces catalog. The books are classified using a slightly modified Library of Congress scheme. While English is the predominant language, there are titles in 85 other tongues. Most books are reference, but there is a collection of 4000 circulating titles for Garden members. The library fields 3000 interlibrary loan requests every year.

Darwin presides over the Rare Books Room.

This library is one more addition to the 100-year club. It was opened to the public in 1900 and has been in continuous operation since. They do not provide e-books, but they have a selection of electronic journals for use in the library. There is an active digitization program for rare materials, and they partner with the Internet Archive, sending books to the Archive's satellite office in Princeton. They are also active in the Digital Public Library of America (DPLA). I confessed that I had looked at the DPLA when it first came live and thought the content was thin. "Look again," I was told.

"This institution is not a passive thing. Real science has gone on here and continues to this day." Sinon told me that both puffed wheat and puffed rice were invented here. Also, seedless grapes were developed at the garden.

I asked where they send people to eat, and Sinon told me that there are two excellent restaurants on the premises. If people want to get away and have their own means, they are not far from a wonderful selection of restaurants on Arthur Avenue.

A month later, my mother-in-law was in from Arizona, and we needed someplace unique to take her. I joined the New York Botanical Gardens and we spent an excellent afternoon riding the trolley and reacquainting ourselves with the Gardens. Afterward, we ate at the Garden's main restaurant and we can confirm that it is a very classy place to spend an afternoon.

FURTHER READING

Article about the Gardener's Dictionary: http://www.london.umb.edu/index.php/entry_detail/philip_millers_gardeners_dictionary/commerce/.

Channel Thirteen WNET tour of the New York Botanical Society Library with Stephen Sinon: http://www.thirteen.org/program-content/the-new-york-botanical-garden-mertz-library-tour/.

Digital Public Library of America: http://dp.la/.

E.O. Wilson page: http://eowilsonfoundation.org/e-o-wilson/.

Internet Archive: http://archive.org.

Miller's Dictionary of Gardening revised: https://books.google.com/books/about/Miller_s_dictionary_of_gardening_botany.html?id=5z4AAAAAQAAJ.

Monticello Gardens: http://www.monticello.org/site/house-and-gardens/historic-gardens.

AFTERWORD

Tuesday mornings at Gill Library were something I always looked forward to. That's when I met with Terry Ballard over coffee and he would tell me about his most recent library journey through New York City for his book *50 Specialty Libraries in New York City*. The stories kept me in awe, because all I knew was my local library and the main branch of The New York Public Library, and here was this Arizonan telling me, a native New Yorker, about these marvelously unique libraries that are right under my nose.

Terry told me about The Players Club, founded in 1888 by American actor Edwin Booth. Though Edwin rarely, if ever, spoke of his infamous brother, John Wilkes Booth, he did have his brother's photo by his bedside. Then there is the New York Society Library, which was founded in 1754 under a charter from King George III. One of the library's famous patrons was George Washington, who, by the way, still owes a late fee.

I asked Terry about the criteria of selecting libraries for *50 Specialty Libraries in New York City*, and he simply stated that the libraries needed to be somewhat accessible, interesting, and unique. It was also interesting to hear from Terry that many of the libraries he visited are aware that they are as not well known as they think they should be. He wanted to give people "a sense of the enormous variety of services available to the interested researcher besides the traditional well-known system in New York City."

In asking the author about what inspired him to research and write a book about unique libraries, he mentioned the author Marilyn Johnson, and her book *This Book is Overdue*, who had written about the little-known American Kennel Club Library, so he wondered what other libraries existed in NYC. Places such as the Masonic Library, the Hispanic Society Library, and the Xavier Society for the Blind, which houses Helen Keller's writing desk and Oscar award and where, on a wall, there is writing from Helen's hand that mentions her meeting with Mark Twain and that "I have met a king," and that just by touching him she felt his humanity. At the Explorer's Club Terry's mind was blown, seeing the table where they began planning the Panama Canal and where a piece of Thor Heyerdahl's Kon-Tiki was displayed; Theodore Roosevelt's lantern slides of his honeymoon in Egypt and his explorations of the Amazon are available for viewing. The Conjuring Library for Magicians, where incunabula from the 1400s are displayed absolutely amazed me. Then there is The Poet's House, where one can see the desk of E.E. Cummings.

It took Terry four intense months to investigate all the libraries, and all but two were traveled to via New York City public transportation. Perhaps in the future, Terry Ballard will revise this work to *60 Specialty Libraries in New York City*, because they are certainly out there. He would be delighted to see someone take the time to explore the somewhat obscure and unobserved libraries in Boston, Washington, DC, San Francisco, and Philadelphia. I think everyone will be well served if he continued his work.

—by Kathleen S. Mannino, an academic librarian

INDEX

'*Note:* Page numbers with "f" indicate figures.'

Printed and bound by CPI Group (UK) Ltd, Croydon, CR0 4YY

08/06/2025

01896869-0012